MARIE TAGLIONI

SCENE FROM "LA SYLPHIDE"

From the lithograph after the painting by Lepolle

MARIE TAGLIONI

(1804–1884)

By

ANDRÉ LEVINSON

Translated by

CYRIL W. BEAUMONT

Noverre Press

First published in 1930

This edition published in 2014 by
The Noverre Press
Southwold House
Isington Road
Binsted
Hampshire
GU34 4PH

ISBN 978-1-906830-67-0

To Madame ANNA PAVLOVA

The dancer in whom has entered, for our delight, the spirit of

MARIE TAGLIONI

ACKNOWLEDGMENTS

The present translation has been made from the French original published at Paris, 1929, by the Librairie Félix Alcan. In this connection I should like to record my sincere appreciation of M. André Levinson's kindness in reading through my translation and offering me many helpful suggestions. I am also indebted to my friend Mr. de V. Payen-Payne, who, in addition to overlooking the proofs, afforded me, on several occasions, the benefit of his valuable advice.

C. W. B.

CONTENTS

ILLUSTRATIONS

The head-piece and tail-piece used throughout this book have been designed by Eileen Mayo. The medallion used on the cover is a reduced reproduction of that struck in honour of Marie Taglioni at Milan, 1843.

MARIE TAGLIONI

CHAPTER I

IN THE BEGINNING

" Taglioni, venez, princesse d'Arcadie . . ."
EDGAR DEGAS.

The Legend of the Sylphide—A *débutante* in the light of criticism—The Taglioni Dynasty—Marie Taglioni and the French School—Caravans—Stuttgart, a colony of French ballet—The first portraits of Marie—Pre-romanticism.

MARIE TAGLIONI'S fame is one of the most widespread commonplaces of the era of romanticism. Legend has completely triumphed over fact. Even in 1844 a contemporary declares that " Taglioni was for us—as Terpsichore for the people of the Empire—a whole poem in one word." A literary fiction has coloured the truth regarding this great person ; the lyrical outbursts of poets exalted the Sylphide to the seventh heaven ; the engravings which adorned *Keepsakes* masked her real features beneath a likeness of pure convention. The complex and private life of a human being is submerged under a monotonous and verbose phraseology, because mediocrity in literature had never sunk so low as during the aftermath of 1830. There are references to Taglioni in plenty, but they date from a period but little interested in actuality, which was openly ignored in accordance with the usage of the day. The chronicler of the Romantic era, such as Janin or Arsène Houssaye, distorts and fakes the facts without scruple ; he makes the most of them, sharpens their outlines or stretches them by wordy amplification. The brothers Goncourt had not yet introduced the cult of research and the necessity for sounding the depths of history. It is true that the public, partial to dainty morsels, expected from its entertainers indiscreet details regarding the stars of the day. The sordid Mirecourt dealt in scurrilous gossip and base insinuations. Stories abounded, and advertisement and slander went hand in hand. This gossip became an unhealthy craving ; and when the stock of rumours ran low, others were invented. In short, it was a period akin to our own ; a period greedy for scandal and romantic " lives."

Taglioni, " that other charming angel of imaginary heavens," to quote Théodore de Banville, was also a woman flattered and envied. She did not only interest the poets ; she also contributed her share—however small—to the tittle-tattle. However, she does not figure among the great lovers nor among the " *filles de l'Opéra* " who flit through the pages of the secret memoirs of the eighteenth century. Scandal has no real hold on so meritorious a life, full of hard work and high ambition. Quoted and watered down by lazy searchers, scandal and base suggestion nevertheless were repeated in book after book. Are we better informed regarding the dancer considered to be the greatest of her age ? Hardly ! The kings of journalism completely ignore the dance and confine themselves to florid paraphrases, with the exception of " good Théo,"[1] who was right to call himself " one of those for whom the visible world exists." Such is the extreme difficulty of the biographer who attempts to present a correct, or at least plausible, account of Taglioni. He willingly relinquishes his best effects ; but does not this sacrifice procure him a little indulgence ? We shall devote

[1] Théophile Gautier—*Tr.*

ourselves solely to constructing a true memorial of a great existence.

* * *

" What ? Twenty-five degrees[1] of heat and the house almost full ! " exclaims on August 3rd, 1827, the musical critic of the *Journal des Débats*. " Nevertheless, there is no novelty ; a well-known opera undoubtedly witnessed with pleasure, but seen so many times, and a ballet, the noisiest of all ballets . . ." When one considers the corresponding programme given by the Académie Royale de Musique, one shares the journalist's astonishment. Spontini's *La Vestale*, of which the parody by the popular " *chansonnier*," Désaugiers, alone survives in anthologies, had seen twenty years' service. As for the ballet *Les Filets du Vulcain*, the cyclops overwhelmed the double basses and trombones by striking in rhythm on their anvils. Not for nothing had the composer, Jean Schneitzhoeffer, once been a cymbalist at the Opéra ! And had he not introduced, a deafening bit of audacity, four trumpets into his orchestral score ? More-over, the Paris season was over. The daily papers published odes in celebration of the victory of Navarino ; Sir Walter Scott's *Life of Napoleon* provided the only literary interest ; English actors were to be seen at the Odéon, where they were giving Shakespeare. However, the Rue Le Peletier[2] was crowded. " Do not let us deceive ourselves and hasten to make apologies," exclaims emphatically the writer who signs himself with a C., and who is none other than Castil-Blaze, the prolific lyrical versifier, Rossini's Quinault[3] and adapter of the *Barber*, who since 1820 wielded the critic's whip at the *Débats*. " If the plays were old, a dancer just arrived from Italy was there to infuse new life into them. It is mainly to Mlle. Taglioni that the management owes its success . . ." Having smilingly disposed of the favourable customary formulæ and quoted the indispensable

[1] Centigrade—*Tr.*
[2] The street in which the Opéra was situated—*Tr.*
[3] Lully's librettist.

17

Latin tag, the critic proceeds to a comparison, in order to throw his heroine into relief.

"Every one remembers the elder Mlle. Gosselin and the astonishing flexibility of her limbs, that muscular strength which enabled her to remain posed *sur les pointes* for one or two minutes. . . . Mlle. Gosselin is no more." We know that Mlle. Gosselin, a victim of overwork, died from exhaustion; did not Julien Louis Geoffroy, the arbiter of theatrical taste under the Empire, coin an altogether new word to express her prodigious suppleness? He called her *la désossée*, the boneless one. A century later, Valentin, the can-can dancer at the Ball of the Moulin Rouge, and Toulouse-Lautrec's favourite model, earned the same nickname. . . .

"Mlle. Taglioni," declares Blaze, "seems to be particularly destined to take the place of that excellent dancer. She has much the same height, the same intrepid poses, the same suppleness of movement. Mlle. Taglioni put the seal to her success by the extremely brilliant manner in which she performed a *pas de deux* in the first act of *La Vestale*, and another *pas de deux* added by M. Taglioni *père* to *Les Filets de Vulcain*." As for the newcomer's brother and partner who helped her to shine, the critic reproaches him with "having exceeded the limits of brotherly courtesy." We shall have more to say about that brother, called Paul.

Having pronounced judgment, Castil-Blaze unmasks his batteries and proceeds to theorise; it is from Noverre's *Letters* that he gleans most of his doctrines. So he refuses to found his judgment on these exercises in pure choregraphy.

"Dancing in the true sense of the word . . . (according to him) is only the mechanical side of the art, and even when one has come to excel in it one scarcely merits the title of artist. It is mime, that is to say expression, which alone can warrant the esteem of true connoisseurs." The eloquent critic from Avignon revives the everlasting dispute between dancing and mime, movement and action, form and expression. In support of his opinion, he evokes the example of Mlle. Bigottini, whose glory is lasting, in contrast to so many forgotten leapers ; it is an eloquent reference, since Mlle. Bigottini, having retired four years before, had formerly, when playing in *Nina ou la Folle par Amour*, caused the swordsmen of Wagram to shed tears. And he alleges further the precedent of the Paul family ; the early decline of the husband who " limited himself entirely to a tight-rope walker's exercises," and to the ever-increasing vogue of Mlle. Montessu (*alias* Mme. Paul), whose success in *La Somnambule* counterbalanced in a short time the new fame of Marie Taglioni.

It is in this spirit that the presumptuous hypercritic lectures the dancer. " To avoid such misfortune, Mlle. Taglioni has much to achieve. She is already sufficiently high in the opinion of the public and it rests with her to substitute dramatic parts for the simple *pas* in which up to the present she has merely displayed her physical advantages, and we must wait for that event before we can give a decision." And he asks himself whether she will be found a worthy rival of the Gardels, Bigottini and such other glories of the past whose names awake not the slightest echo in us. His observations on Mlle. Taglioni's physical appearance reduce themselves to the same very summary generalities ; he finds her features expressive and remarks that her gestures are unstudied ; in short, he rather reserves his opinion of a dancer whom he believes to be only eighteen. This is an erroneous deduction which we hasten to correct since it is repeated in many biographies of the illustrious dancer ; other historians are divided between these two dates of birth : 1804 and 1809. The second, favoured by Castil-Blaze, seems to have been devised simply to make the interesting beginner appear still more youthful after a career of five years. But later on we shall deal more fully with Marie Taglioni's antecedents. In the meantime we shall continue the account of her Parisian appearances, keeping to contemporary Press notices, much the more valuable in that they precede both her Parisian and her international fame. Most contemporary criticisms, such as those of Jules Janin or of Théophile Gautier, as well as those contained in the prose and verse anthologies which are continually quoted, are tributes paid to the already celebrated star—variations on a theme known to all. In 1827, romanticist criticism was still unborn ; neither the *Siècle* nor Girardin's *Presse* was in existence ; Alexandre Dumas had not yet wrested the dramatic page from hacks in order to give it to famous authors. Articles signed J. J. had not yet appeared in the *Débats*, nor others signed G. G. (Gautier, and Gérard de Nerval) in the *Presse*. On the other hand, Geoffroy, a critic as careless as he was dictatorial, was dead. Obscure interpreters of a still uncertain verdict, the chroniclers of 1827 were called upon to discover at their risk and peril an unknown genius, a task which in its turn requires no little intelligence. Indeed, it was the public who forced them to prick up their ears. It was the rumour of Mlle. Taglioni's first success on July 23rd which, a week later, drew Castil-Blaze to the Opéra. His reticence and lectures are entitled, nevertheless, to some indulgence. For, five years later, he published a work entitled *La Danse et les Ballets,* " *depuis Bacchus jusqu'à Mlle. Taglioni,*" from Bacchus to Mlle. Taglioni, a sufficient indication that he regarded the latter name of particular importance in the history of the art.

Let us be all the more just to the vigilance of his anonymous colleague on the *Constitutionel* who, on the morning of July 23rd, in a paragraph on *La Somnambule,* which is the principal attraction at the end of the season, incidentally announces " two dancing *débuts* : that of M. Taglioni and his sister ; fresh from their successes at Naples ; but, as regards dancing, there is a good deal of difference between French taste and that of the Neapolitan public." In confirmation of this anticipated and somewhat malicious reservation, he mentions a certain Calabrian dance seen at the San Carlo Theatre and which appeared too intoxicating to the Parisians ; it is the chaste Marie who excites all these apprehensions ! Other observations by the same critic make us shudder. Does he not declare that " solo dancing seems to me as extravagant as scenery seen apart from the play " ? However, the carper will be unable to resist Taglioni's charm.

MARIE TAGLIONI
From the lithograph by Leon Noël

In his article of the 28th,[1] he again compares Paul with Marie, to the detriment of the former. He criticises the young man rather severely; he finds him feeble and not manly enough, he discovers further that he turns in an " unusual " manner. " M. Taglioni's sister," he continues, in a more enthusiastic vein, " is likewise tall and thin; the undulations of her body, at once slender and rounded, are quite in harmony with the movements of her neck, her head, her arms, her legs and her feet; the general effect is supple and graceful; however, this is not the grace with which we are acquainted; it has an air of originality, of strangeness even, without being wild or countrified. Mlle. Taglioni's features present a type of beauty which has nothing in common with that of France; her big eyes, wide-opened and somewhat staring, hold the spectators charmed and spellbound. The occupants of the stalls at the Opéra have lost the habit of, but not the taste for, novelties; they stamped with joy. . . . I have seldom witnessed such brilliant *débuts* in dancing as those of Mlle. and M. Taglioni.

It was in *Le Sicilien*, a mediocre ballet[2] adapted by A. Petit from Molière's comedy, in which Louis XIV. used to dance the final *entrée*, that Marie Taglioni made her first appearance at the Opéra. I agree that the *Constitutionel's* praise seems thin and its expressions weak from over use. The critic lacks both the necessary knowledge and an appropriate vocabulary to record his impressions. But his good sense enables him to recognise at the first glance, if not to define, Marie Taglioni's originality and the suggestive or rather hypnotic power of her art. The public

[1] Charles Maurice, the dreaded editor of the *Courier des Théâtres*, who patronised Taglioni's engagement, will have preceded him; on the 24th he comments on her appearance in these terms : " This young lady's features present a happy combination of natural gifts; beautiful eyes, a noble and touching manner with considerable charm in this graceful whole. As for dancing, Mlle. Taglioni is a ravishing combination of all that is seductive and out of the ordinary in this art." Her inconceivable performance would have abounded in new and difficult things wherein her sureness and balance would be demonstrated. Five years later he will violently attack his illustrious *protégée*; we shall speak again of this newspaper war.

[2] The score is by Ferdinand Sor, the dance music by Schneitzhœffer.

was carried away by it; we must thank the critic for not having believed it to be his duty to resist the popular judgment. In a fortnight and after seven performances, Taglioni's reputation is made. Did not Duponchel, the young architect attached to the staff of the Opéra, of which he was one day to be the director, inaugurate a charming custom by throwing a bouquet[1] on the stage? Having appeared in Albert's *Cendrillon* and received a thousand bravos, Taglioni introduced into Spontini's *Fernand Cortez* "*un pas de schal*" (*sic*) which achieved a furore. "It is impossible to convey an idea of what the dancer has made of the *pas de schal*, before this the figures had seemed so hackneyed that they could never be used again. One would have liked to see that other Gosselin take shape once more, and drape and wind herself in her light scarf, cast it away and reappear freed of that voluptuous fetter, and then as suddenly lose herself in it anew and, forsaking it, become, as though by magic, grace united to modesty."

And the correspondent hastens to refute the calumny which attributes to Aumer the composition of this *pas* bearing the sign-manual of Taglioni *père*.

Mlle. Taglioni bade the Parisians farewell on August 10th, this time definitely, in a *pas* added to *Le Carnaval de Venise*; already her name sufficed to draw a crowd. She is about to leave for Munich. Will she return? It will be a difficult matter to manage. She insists on a salary calculated to exasperate the legitimate covetousness of her rivals, the Noblets and the Montessus. But does she not henceforth take her place " in the first rank of the dancers of the age " ? And so she is engaged for the period of eight years ; the agreement will be settled after three months' negotiations, as is evident from a letter of Taglioni *père* to Charles Maurice, the famous filibuster of the theatrical Press. And the critic of the *Constitutionel* once more pronounces (*Nouvelles de Théâtre*, August 13th) judgment on the " new Terpsichore." " In the airs, graces and talent of Mlle. Taglioni there is a kind of modesty and

[1] Or rather a garland of white flowers. " Everyone in the house would have liked to have woven this garland," says Ch. Maurice.

artlessness which makes them beyond price ; and then her dances are new ; we have seen no one dance as she does."

Unfortunately for us, the critic is unable to define this difference in concrete and palpable terms. But as regards Taglioni's style, her manner of being, he goes right to the heart of the matter ; modesty and artlessness. He recognises the spiritual quality of her art ; others develop this theme to infinity. From her first appearance at Paris, Marie Taglioni takes her place in the history of the theatre. Her apprenticeship is at an end, her personality is formed. But to arrive at a true appreciation of this personality, we must delve into her beginnings, the growth of her talent and her rise to fame. Documentary matter is not altogether lacking. It will enable us to place the personage who astonished her contemporaries so prodigiously. What strikes our minds as being the " spontaneous development " of a new art is nothing but the last stage of an evolution.

* * *

The wandering tribe of Taglionis, to which " Marie of many graces " belonged, was fecund and prosperous. It is a peculiarity of families that uphold a living tradition and an unbroken continuity to produce a series of artistes who transmit from father to son the secrets of a calling, the processes of execution, the fusion of complex and imponderable elements which constitute a style. Witness the famous dynasties that ruled over the art of ballet : that of the Vestris which lasted for two centuries and shone from the Seven Years' War[1] to the July Monarchy[2] ; that of the Petipas, a family of dancers originating from Marseille, a branch of which was called to direct the destinies of theatrical dancing in Russia ; and lastly that of the Taglionis. It is curious to notice how these dynasties generally expire with the third generation, and that the second of the name generally attains to the height of renown ; then the family genius declines towards medi-ocrity ; it was the same with the Taglionis. Philippe,

[1] 1748—Tr.   [2] 1830—Tr.

the founder of the dynasty, avoided oblivion through his daughter Marie. This Philippe was of Milanese extraction ; he had been *maître de ballet* at the Theatre Royal, Stockholm[1] ; there he married the daughter of a Swedish singer called Carsten ; the result of this union was Marie, born on April 24th, 1804. These facts, fully established, have sufficed to make him pass for an Italian master matured among Northern mists in a Scandinavian *ultima Thule*. As a result of this crossing of two races, Marie appeared doubly foreign to that French circle which she was destined to enchant. She would have been a flower of romantic exotism such as Fanny Elssler, Lucile Grahn or Lola Montès. She was regarded as strange, mysterious ; and people loved to think of her as a foreigner ; it was a mistake. Marie Taglioni is much the greatest glory of the French school, and occupied the same position as that formerly held by a Camargo or a Gætano Vestris, despite their foreign origin. Her father, Philippe, had long been attached to the staff of the Opéra ; he did not cut a great figure there, but he was not unnoticed. Geoffroy, in an account of the *Noces de Gamache,* arranged by Milon, gives a flattering description of the villagers' *entrée* danced by Philippe and three of his comrades (30 *Nivôse,* year IX.). Philippe also took part in *La Dansomanie* (1800) and, two years later, in *Le Retour de Zéphyre.* Passing in review " the excellent dancers " who have left the Opéra, Noverre, in the final edition of his *Letters* (1807), having cited Bauvillier, Didelot and others, adds briefly : " Lastly Taglioni and his sister in Italy." We notice therefore that while our man is mentioned last, he is classed with the *best.* Would the wandering dancer in the course of his journeys have renounced the French tradition and have embraced the genial heresies of Vigano, the inventor of the " choreodrama " ? We have no reason to think so, since Philippe is reprimanded by Stendhal for being too

[1] Born in 1781, the son of Carlo Taglioni, an obscure dancer, he was also *maître de ballet* at Cassel, which post he received from King Jerome ; he ended his career at Warsaw in 1853, and died at Como on February 11th, 1871. Salvador Taglioni, who founded a Royal School of Dancing at Naples in 1812, is a namesake of Philippe's.

much of a Frenchman. In a footnote on Duport's benefit at the San Carlo Theatre, Naples (*Rome, Naples et Florence*, under the date March 2nd, 1817), "Arrigo Beyle, *Milanese*," once more attacks the coldness of French dancing. While not criticising Duport who "amuses him just as a kitten does," he imputes "that coldness and those courtier-like graces" to Mme. Duport, Taglioni and Mlle. Taglioni (Louise, Marie's aunt; she made her last appearance at the Opéra in 1806, in *La Caravane du Caire*). It must therefore be concluded that no appreciable difference in Philippe's style was noticeable on his return from Sweden. Moreover, Philippe had not always been his daughter's sole mentor. She even went to Paris, and at the age of eight it would appear that she was the pupil of the elder Coulon, patriarch of the professors who also trained Mlles. Montessu and Gosselin. At those sought-after evenings given by the venerable pedagogue to display the products of his method, one saw all the celebrities of the Opéra. Thus Marie's art was the result of the same training which produced the pick of the French dancers. And at this period French choregraphy was so universal that she will make her *début* at Vienna beside Mlle. Millière, a former member of the Opéra, the very Millière, according to old Noverre, whose "irregular but unusually pleasing features," and whose "brilliant and vigorous dancing" counterbalanced her ignorance of music. All these ties clearly connect Marie Taglioni with the time-honoured tradition of the School. Her personality does not transgress the confines of French dancing. She anticipated and guided its natural and logical development.

But these general views are too premature at this stage, for we are still dealing with Taglioni's early introductions to theatrical life. The *Wiener Theater-Zeitung* gives us a sympathetic account of what these were:—

"Yesterday was the first performance of a new anacreontic ballet arranged by M. Taglioni, the Imperial and Royal *maître de ballet*, in which appeared for the first time Mlle. Marie Taglioni, a young person of the highest ability. . . . Her pleasing features, her graceful movements, the convincing quality of her technical perfection already make her an accomplished dancer and show her capable of still further development. . . . The public accorded her a favourable reception which she well deserved." Philippe knew how to invest his daughter's first appearance with flattering allegory and symbolic allusion : for theme, he had chosen a young nymph's reception at Terpsichore's court (*La Réception d'une Jeune Nymphe à la Cour de Terpsichore*) ; this mythological *entrée* served to bring the new-comer in opposition to Mlle. Millière, already mentioned, and Mlle. Héberle, celebrated for her beauty ; this juxtaposition did not harm the young dancer in the least, quite the contrary. A second piece brought the same artistes together in a *pas de trois*, the success of which mitigated the failure of the ballet adapted by Henri (a French *maître de ballet*, whom the crusty Noverre had formerly dissuaded from the " composition of ballets, an exhausting occupation, bad for the health ") from Shakespeare's *Hamlet*, duly watered down, the music for which was composed by Comte Gallemberg. The first campaigns on behalf of romanticism were scarcely victorious as regards ballet, least of all at the Kaernther-Thor,[1] nevertheless we must pay tribute to Henri's courage, up till then responsible for a certain *Amour à Cythère*, the most old-fashioned of ballets ; he made the Prince of Denmark dance seven years before Stendhal's pamphlet[2] and eleven years before the preface to Cromwell.[3]

For two years we lose sight of Taglioni. Her biographers make out that, in 1824, she appeared with little success at the Théâtre de la Porte Saint-Martin; this remains to be proved. The choregraphic activities of that theatre, nicknamed the " People's Opera House," were by no means negligible. Aumer had revived Dauberval's rustic ballets there ; during the Empire he had the

1 This pantomime had had a great success in 1816, as is proved by a letter of Hérold published by M. Julian Tiersot. Mme. Guériau, a celebrated mime, made the success of the piece. " It is criticised, but it makes money, and that is everything."
2 *Racine et Shakespeare—Tr.*
3 By Victor Hugo, published 1828—*Tr.*

MARIE TAGLIONI
From the lithograph drawn from life by Vigneron

temerity to put on his *Deux Créoles*, adapted from the
romance by Bernardin de Saint-Pierre, in opposition to
Pierre Gardel's *Paul et Virginie*, staged at the Opéra;
we see Geoffroy compare the two versions. The *maître
de ballet* Hullin and his childish quadrilles were the rage
of the boulevards. We have been unable to find a single
trace of Taglioni's supposed unfortunate appearance at
this theatre where shone Mmes. Alexis, Juliette and Floren-
tine; perhaps other searchers will be more successful
than ourselves. For this period we lack both references
and pictorial documents which her renown was destined
to bring forth in plenty between 1830 and 1840; some
caricatures regarding her Viennese period afford but a
meagre source of information. We are more fortunate
in regard to her stay at Stuttgart. Some important recollections connect the capital of Wurtemberg with the
history of French dancing. There Jean Georges Noverre
had held despotic sway; for six years Stuttgart was the
Mecca of ballet-pantomime. There came the great Vestris
to be initiated in the new doctrine. The anecdotic history
of Taglioni describes at great length the royal favours
enjoyed by the dancer, which in the case of the queen
rose to the height of the closest friendship. "Were you
my sister I could not be more sad at your leaving me."
Such are the touching words which unrefuted legend has
attributed to Her Majesty. Moreover, the officious
biographers of the Sylphide never forgot to mention the
esteem in which various monarchs held Taglioni. Nothing
impresses the man in the street more than this type of halo;
however, we have no space here to question the veracity
of such reports. The prestige of her talent and her dignified
personality conferred on Marie Taglioni a regal air before
which even royalty bowed the head.

Fortunately for the seeker, there is pictorial evidence
to corroborate anecdote. A very rare album of six
coloured lithographs: *Souvenirs sur les Ballets au Théâtre
Royal de Stuttgart*, dated 1826, contains, despite the artlessness of the drawings, valuable information. I had the
portfolio in my possession for a very brief period. But

the late Nicholas Soloviev, the *balletomane* and eminent bibliophile, and Taglioni's Russian biographer, has given some reduced reproductions of them in his excellent book. The first plate depicts Marie Taglioni dancing a *pas de deux* with young Stuhlmuller (who, in four years' time was to be Fanny Elssler's partner in Berlin and the hero of a love affair with the beautiful Viennese), in *Zémire et Azor*, a ballet presented at the Paris Opéra in 1824, and making use of a theme employed more than fifty years earlier by Marmontel and Grétry. In the Shawl Dance in *Le Soirée d'un Rajah* she has her brother Paul for partner, and Signor Turchetto in an *entrée* from *La Foire*.

The first two plates mentioned show Taglioni in *temps d'adage*. Raised *sur la pointe* she executes some *équilibres* combined with ample *développés*, her raised and rounded arms supporting the movement. Despite the blunders of the artist, who ignores the mechanism of the legs turned *en dehors*, we recognise the rigid vertical of the perpendicular ending in the *pointe*. The great romantic line is thus realised : the leg stretched, the *cou de pied* forced outwards, the sole " broken." In the *Rajah* plate, the star executes a *tour de pirouette*. In *Zémire*, as in *La Foire*, a *divertissement* in the comic opera manner, of which Dauberval's *La Fille Mal Gardée* is the prototype, the play of the veil or scarf serves as pretext or accessory for the *pas de deux* ; it envelops and swells the slender linear armature.

Thus in *La Foire*, Taglioni balances herself *en attitude sur la pointe*, holding with her finger-tips the edge of the scarf which her partner, stationed at a little distance behind her, draws to him. All these dance themes, although cruelly deformed by the delineator's flagrant inability, foreshadow the Sylphide's silhouette as true artists such as Devéria and Chalon are to symbolise her ten years hence. Even the costume, although overburdened with embroidered motifs in the *Rajah* and with " appliqué " palm-leaves in *Zémire*, proceeds towards the lily-like uniform devised by Eugène Lami for the Sylphide. The close-fitting bodice, outlining her delicate and rounded figure, modestly uncovers her neck ; the sleeves, very short and full, suggest epaulettes. The light and very full skirt falls a little above the knee. Her wavy hair, gathered in bands, bares a portion of her forehead; her neck is long, her head small. Already we distinguish the intangible being of legend, the human frame impelled towards its most abstract expression, its mass reduced to the play of straight lines and pure curves. The style of this dress, which will soon be universal at the Opéra, is ever so slightly modified in the *pas de quatre* called *L'Epée et la Lance* which opposes—a pyrrhic executed in the manner of David—Amazons to Greek warriors; the helmet with visor and plume is intended to accord the dancers a martial air.

A different document, likewise emanating from Stuttgart, shows us Marie Taglioni in the very year of her first appearances at Paris. It is a lithograph by F. Lauter in which we admire the "model maiden" in her dress of stiff muslin, scarcely baring her neck; neither jewels nor lace disturb the almost nun-like severity and virginal modesty of this picture. We recognise the locks which the Sylphide will shortly discard for a different head-dress: smooth bands, the forehead revealed by the hair drawn back and done up in a knot at the nape of the neck. But it is not the butterfly which we are discussing now; it is the chrysalis.

We shall find her again in Paris. Fêted at Munich by the poet-king whose throne will presently be shaken by another dancer, Lola Montès, petitioned by Italy, what does she seek at the Opéra? There was a vacancy to be filled there. One by one the stars which shone during the Empire had vanished. Mlle. Clotilde[1] died in 1825, she forsook the stage in 1818; Mlle. Bigottini retired five years later. Marie Taglioni dares to aim at succeeding

[1] Clotilde Malfleuroy, who had married Boïeldieu, remains celebrated in the annals of gallantry. If Mlle. Georges was called " a beautiful statue," Mlle. Clotilde was termed " a beautiful creature." Nestor Roqueplan in 1855 heard admirers still talking of a certain indescribable movement of the hips which gave Clotilde's entire body a tremor of unutterable voluptuousness. This blonde with blue eyes was affected with a sad infirmity: when she danced she emitted a disagreeable odour.

these two stars. Does she come to announce a new epoch ? She rather tends to carry on the still unexpressed spirit of a period which declines towards to its end. She belongs to the decade of *Les Méditations*, not to that of *Les Orientales*. The July monarchy will set up Fanny Elssler, the Spaniard from the North. Marie Taglioni is as far removed from sensual ardour as from the drama of passion ; she embodies an idea : that of the Restoration. The pure white of her tunic is something more than a personal whim. She displays the Bourbon colours ; the return to white, to the misty splendour of transparent muslin, corresponds to a universal infatuation. Similarly, the classic heel-less ballet-shoe is a derivation of the slipper worn by the exquisites on their return from Gent. Elssler will be the carnation of Granada, Taglioni is the fleur-de-lis. The technique of tradition becomes the language of the ineffable. This transformation of gymnastic movement strikes people's minds with astonishment. We have seen criticism disabled, incapable of explaining, indeed, unable to reduce the strangeness of this art to a formula, the announcement made by Marie. At first, she had brought nothing new ; not a single manifesto announced her ideas. She submissively took one by one the different parts in the repertory. For five years she did not create a single new ballet, and scarcely a rôle in an opera-ballet by Scribe. But what, thanks to her, is achieved, is the interior illumination of a style. The traditional dance had been an exercise pleasant to witness ; henceforth, it expressed the things of the soul ; the ballet was an entertainment ; it became a mystery. Writers ill-informed as regards the history of dancing endeavour to contrast the romantic dance with the classic dance.

The antithesis is arbitrary. In reality, the new style is superimposed on the old one. The revolution marks the climax of tradition. This, however, is a premature revelation, since our intention is still only to show the Sylphide on the eve of her fame, just as she appeared to those who ignored what the future held for her.

CHAPTER II

THE FLIGHT

" Un bel oiseau ne suivrait pas
Tes pas."

JOUY AND BIS.

Ballet at the Opéra in 1827—The Tyrolienne of *Guillaume Tell*—
Le Dieu et la Bayadère—Rivalries—Perrot the Aerial—Dr. Véron's
management—The cloister of *Robert le Diable*—The Infernal
Valse.

" OH 1827," the poet[1] of *Albertus* will cry out ten years
later, " period of overrunning verses, of local
colour, of philhellenes, where art thou ? As far away
as the reign of Sesotris or that of the Pharaoh Meneptah ;
vanished, alas, with our golden youth and our beautiful
springtide illusions." And he begins to pity the crude
and antediluvian ballets of that distant age ! Now the
majority of the ballets in which Marie Taglioni shone in
1827 were already recollections of the Empire, ballets
somewhat out of fashion at the time of her first appearance.
The polished metal helmets made in 1809 for the dancers
in *Fernand Cortez* must have been somewhat rusty, and the
tinsel of Jouy and Castel's *Bayadères* as faded as possible.
Taglioni, moreover, does not form a part of these worn-
out productions. At first, she only intervenes in the
entrées or *pas de deux* interpolated in those pieces ; her
father devises these *hors d'œuvre*. Having returned to the

[1] Théophile Gautier—*Tr.*

Opéra on April 30th, 1828, she reappeared only once during three years, in an episodic *pas*. Although henceforth " all spoke as one for Taglioni and everyone was enchanted, ravished,"[1] her personal success could not avert the failure of *Lydie* which Castil-Blaze unkindly designates as a mythological drollery, a drollery most certainly not intended. Not until a year later does Taglioni take her revenge. On July 23rd, 1829, she lends her support to the 925th performance of *Psyche*, by Pierre Gardel, given for the benefit of the venerable *chorégraphe*, a glorious relic of the eighteenth century. This ballet in three acts, first produced in 1790, delighted Henri Beyle in 1804 ; but when the art of Salvator Vigano was revealed to him, the theorist of romanticism reverted from this youthful infatuation. Nothing was omitted to heighten the splendour of that solemn occasion. Schneitzhœffer was asked to modernise the music. And the scene on Olympus served once more as a pretext for a ceremony similar to that which had succeeded so well at Vienna ; the investiture of the dancer Taglioni and her presentation to Terpsichore, embodied in Mme. Anatole (the younger Gosselin), who invites her to prove her merit.

Obstinately, she keeps to pure dancing ; she appears only in impersonal and, so to speak, abstract parts, independent of the dramatic action. Thus she enters at the head of a band of naiads in *La Belle au Bois Dormant* arranged by Scribe (" a long, slow, heavy and wearisome " ballet, says Castil-Blaze). Ossian and Sir Walter Scott are not yet in fashion. It is old Perrault who satisfied the demand for the fantastic which began to ferment the imagination. If it be a question of supernatural visions, antique mythology is called upon to supply the elements for it. This does not prevent the paradoxical *pas de deux* of Prince Charming with the Naiad, arranged by Aumer to Hérold's music, from procuring Taglioni an extension of contract. The royal management wished to ensure her services for fifteen years. However, a new musical epoch at the Opéra is

---

[1] " In Paris, and outside Paris, everyone spoke of her glory." quotes Charles Maurice.

MARIE TAGLIONI
From the painting by Ary Scheffer
(Musée de Versailles)

about to begin. Rossini's star attains its zenith. Meyer-beer, already acclaimed at Louvois, enters the lists.

Le Comte Ory was praised to the skies. In 1823, Stendhal had lauded the genius of the " swan of Pesaro."

" Since the death of Napoleon," he stated, " another man has been found who is daily the subject of conversation at both Moscow and Naples, at both London and Vienna, at both Paris and Calcutta." And he insisted that Rossini should come to Paris for two years. Two years later this dream was realised. And Rossini composes his greatest and last work—*Guillaume Tell*—for the Académie Royale de Musique. Thenceforth, having no further need of success and being undesirous of exposing himself to failure, the maestro gave himself up to an invincible indolence. In the meanwhile the " inspector-general of singing in France " was supreme at the Opéra ; he was the close adviser of the director, the insignificant Lubbert.

He had been able to appreciate Marie Taglioni in a *pas* added by her to his *Siège de Corinth*. It is for her and Mme. Montessu that he composes the famous Tyrolienne in *Guillaume Tell*, that *chanson dansée* as we should say nowadays :—

> *Un bel oiseau ne suivrait pas*
> *Tes pas !*

So sang the chorus *a capella*, and to that air, accented by voices only, Taglioni and her companion leaped in their mountain dance, a transposition of a popular air into classic steps. If the intention were good, the echoed verses were mediocre. A contemporary asserts that the authors Jouy and Bis (Jouy was the fortunate librettist of *La Vestale* and the writer of *L'Ermite de la Chaussée d'Antin*) were the first to laugh at them. Rossini took it upon himself to replace in one of the verses the word *aiglon* (eaglet), to which the dancer was compared, by *oiseau* (bird), because an eaglet did not seem to him to be associated with dancing. It is true that the audacity of the production caused the audience to forget the massacre of Schiller's tragedy by Jouy and Bis, who were out and out pseudo-classics. Encouraged by Duponchel, Ciceri

33

varied the Alpine scene by adding practicable scaffoldings ; at the end of each tableau the curtain had to be lowered, which had never been done before. The one and only precedent was employed in *La Muette de Portici*, before the climax, in order to prepare for the eruption of Vesuvius. And, a thing unheard of, four trumpeters were added to strengthen the brass band. Mlle. Taglioni did not figure in the cast of Auber's opera which, two years later, was to serve at Brussels as a prologue to the Revolution of 1830. The libretto included the character of a mute, that of Fenella, the unfortunate sister of the fisherman Masaniello, the Neapolitan who revolted against Spanish tyranny. This part was destined to become the touchstone of mimes. Mlle. Lise Noblet had created the touching character of the victim who saves her infamous seducer ; she triumphed in this new style, and it was owing to her success that Marie Taglioni was converted to mime.

Le Dieu et la Bayadère is the counterpart of *La Muette de Portici*, born of a rivalry which is the prologue to the famous quarrel between the Taglionists and the Elsslerists ; a little later this debate was to divide all Paris, just as formerly the Bouffons'[1] quarrel had moved court and town. Having the same Auber for composer they fought with like weapons. Eugène Scribe, the author of both *libretti*, contrived beautiful opportunities for dancing. Curiously enough, he transported to the stage the mute competition between the two dancers ; his work gained greatly by it ; the mixture prescribed by him resuscitated the type of opera-ballet formerly dethroned by ballet-pantomime according to Noverre ; dancing became once more an element mingled with the action expressed by the singers ; each *pas* was the outcome of the situation. With this intention the author of *Le Mariage de Raison* adapted to his purpose Goethe's sublime ballad. The future idol of the " golden mean " reduced to the scale of his own sense of the theatre the theme of Wolfgang-Apollo, as Heinrich Heine styled the Olympian of Weimar. Guided by his knowledge of the theatre and his technical ability, Scribe

---

[1] The struggle between French Opera and Italian *Opera-buffa*.

sought to dramatise the myth of the *bayadère*, redeemed by love and sacrifice from the funeral-pyre by the aid of her divine lover. In the opera-ballet two *bayadères* contest for the favours of the mysterious guest, Zoloë-Taglioni and Néala-Noblet. There is an actual competition. During Néala's *variation*, Zoloë, believing herself disdained by Brahma, has difficulty in concealing her feelings at her unrequited love. In tears, with tenderly clasped hands, she begins to dance in her turn. Again the dark Noblet will incarnate, in *La Sylphide*, Effie, the earthly rival of the winged shade.

La Bayadère amounts to a preliminary sketch in the Taglionesque manner. Fenella was a mimed part pure and simple ; her interpreter neither danced nor even took part in the Neapolitan *divertissement* performed by the *corps de ballet*. Zoloë mimes and dances.[1] Her gestures, however, merely correspond to a recitative. But by means of dancing she expresses the poor girl's exalted love for the divine stranger. Emotion is transposed into the language of the dance ; her steps are supplied by her father who arranged the dances. One hundred and fifty performances attest the success of the experiment.

When, fourteen years later, Marie Taglioni revives this part in which, in 1831, she had been replaced by Mlle. Julia, and, afterwards, by Louise Fitz-James, a prodigy of thinness, Théophile Gautier will take the opportunity to discuss the libretto and even the conception of the opera-ballet.

" Goethe's ballad," he writes, on June 10th, 1844, in his column in the *Presse*, " is a poetic masterpiece ; it might have been written by a Brahmin in the Grottoes of Elephanta . . . so greatly did this powerful genius possess the faculty for assimilation. His supreme fantasy overran

---

[1] Zoloë is not dumb, but, coming from a distant land, she understands the Indian language, although unable to speak it. On this somewhat questionable premise, Taglioni's miming depends. The judge questions her in a song ; he askes her what her profession is. Zoloë replies with a series of *jetés-battus*. What is her consolation in the hour of grief ? A *pas de rigaudon* followed by an *entrechat*, and so forth. In the same way M. Paul Dukas has introduced a barbaric slave as a dumb person in his *Ariane et Barbe Bleue*.

all times and all countries. . . . It is well known that
M. Scribe, despite his wonderful skill, has not been able
to extract everything possible from that delightful legend.
A certain irony penetrates his libretto throughout, and it
is seen that he had not complete faith in the mysterious
tritvam. . . . The mute character of the *bayadère*, in con-
junction with the action which persons sing or speak,
offers certain difficulties which a piece contrived entirely
in pantomime would not possess. Often the character
must hold the stage with nothing to do, while the others
give vent to trills and flourishes. This mixture of con-
ventions produces a disagreeable effect. It may well be
conceded that, by looking at things from a certain angle,
singing and dancing can be the means of expression of a
certain group of persons ; but this is more difficult of
acceptance when a reply expressed in dancing is made to
a question that is sung. Harmony is destroyed, and you
are brought back to reality." Having made his point,
the poet admits that Mlle. Taglioni has overcome this
obstacle " with an infinite good fortune and skill. By
the expressive and touching play of her features in all
manner of ways she links herself with the action that
forsakes her, and demonstrates that she understands every
word the actors say, although they do not speak the same
tongue."

On the other hand, the future librettist of *Sakountala*
criticises the conventional character of the costumes, the
white gauze tunics and pale lemon-coloured tights. Nevertheless, Hippolyte Lecomte's designs preserved at the
Bibliothèque de l'Opéra reveal a remarkably correct feeling
for the period. Were his suggestions followed ? A lithograph shows us the god attired as a comic-opera Turk
wearing an enormous turban. Zoloë-Taglioni, crowned
with flowers and very low-necked, wears on her arms and
ankles broad bracelets in the Hindu manner. No trace of
make-up detracts from the lily-like whiteness of her
features. Liquorice juice, brown silk stockings and cotton
gloves are reserved for the *corps de ballet*, making them
look like chimney-sweeps.

However great her success had been up till then, Mlle. Taglioni remained isolated in her style, which inclined naturally towards elevation, in both the technical and spiritual senses. Since Duport's retirement, the Opéra lacked male dancers able to partner a dancer of her powers of elevation. Thus Perrot's first appearance on January 23rd, 1830, aroused the greatest enthusiasm.[1] This pupil of Vestris inaugurated a style of execution much in keeping with Mlle. Taglioni's dancing. From his first steps, he showed himself worthy of her and merited the surname of "aerial." In *Flore et Zéphyre* the pair eclipsed the memory of Duport and his sister.

Portraits of Perrot are rare. A spiteful whim of destiny had given him a displeasing face and the angular features of a Kalmuk. A similar calamity had driven Didelot to take up choregraphy. Perrot struggled before following his example. Théophile Gautier sketches the great dancer's portrait in a few lines. We shall quote further from this poet pulling an oar in the newspaper galley. The "impeccable master of French letters," according to the words of Charles Baudelaire, is nowadays treated lightly on the strength of a sally by M. André Gide. However that may be, the dance historian is indebted to the plastic prose of the contributor to the *Presse*, to his versatility and appreciative sense, for the ability to conjure up speaking likenesses of the dancers of the past, prose portraits that evoke the immediate and precise vision of the object described. "Perrot is not handsome," he frankly asserts in his article of March 2nd, 1840; "he is extremely ugly. From the waist upwards he has the proportions of a tenor, there is no need to say more; but, from the waist downwards, he is delightful. . . . It hardly accords with modern views to discourse on a man's physical proportions; however, we cannot keep silent regarding Perrot's legs. The foot and knee joints are unusually slender and counterbalance the somewhat feminine roundness of contour of his legs; they are at once soft and strong, elegant

---

[1] Perrot had become known first at the Gaité, then at the Porte Saint Martin Theatre.

and supple, the legs of the youth in red trunks, who breaks
the symbolic wand across his knee in Raphael's painting
The Marriage of the Virgin, are quite in the same style. Let
us add that Perrot . . . has nothing of that feeble and
inane manner which, as a rule, makes male dancers so
tiresome . . . it was not difficult to recognise in the quiet
agility, the perfect rhythm and easy grace of the dancer's
miming, Perrot the aerial, Perrot the sylph, Perrot the male
Taglioni ! "

Did daily training in class suffice to produce this prodigy
of lightness ? Before he became a dancer at the Opéra,
Perrot had been a strolling player ; he willingly admitted
that he had been " Polichinel for three years and a monkey
for two." His wonderful muscles had been strengthened
by his apprenticeship as an acrobat.

Did Perrot discover a kindred soul in her whose style so
closely resembled his own ? Did the suppressed jealousy
that was to burst forth four years later exist from the begin-
ning ? We do not know. But from 1840 Perrot linked
his destiny with that of another dancer, Carlotta Grisi, the
girl with the violet eyes. She became his pupil, then his
wife. Riquet with the Tuft marries the princess, Azor
touches Zémire's heart! The union does not last, it en-
dures but a little while after the decisive triumphs of
Giselle.

However, events are precipitated.[1] The Restoration
melts away before the sun of the July Revolution. The
effects of the revolution make themselves felt at the Opéra ;
the fatherly government instituted by the Vicomte Sosthène
de la Rochefoucauld, the inflexible purist who lengthened
the dancers' skirts by a third, is supplanted by a new order.[2]
The management of the Académie Nationale de Musique is
taken over by Dr. Véron, a Parisian of the middle-class,

[1] On May 3rd, 1830, Taglioni took part in the ballet in *Manon
Lescaut.*

[2] If Nestor Roqueplan's amusing pamphlet, *Les Coulisses de l'Opéra,*
can be credited, that honest and unintelligent autocrat, who had
established two staircases, one for men, the other for women, had not
been able to avoid scandal. Mlle. Julia's virtue, it is asserted, had been
unable to resist his pleading.

MARIE TAGLIONI IN " LA SYLPHIDE "
From the lithograph by A. E. Chalon

who paints his own portrait in his *Mémoires*, and in whom
the self-sufficiency of the upstart does not obscure the fact
that he possessed an abundant stock of commonsense.
This man of business, " a kind of financier of art and
literature," to quote Saint-Beuve, is pompous rather than
open-handed. He spares no effort to dazzle the new
reigning class with sumptuous performances. He will be
accused of having favoured the spectacular side of opera
at the expense of the lyric art. Castil-Blaze will readily
trounce this circus-opera. The doctor, born shrewd, will
rely on the paid *claque* in the gallery and on the publicity
given by the minor newspapers. The very incarnation of
the Balzacian Andoche Finot, he will exploit the credulity
of the public in a masterly way. But this stout and comic
personage possessed in the highest degree a sense of
the theatre and the instinct for success. " He was a
perfect opportunist," remarks one of his detractors. Just
like Baron Taylor at the Comédie Française, he knew how
to surround himself with worthy collaborators. Under
his management, design in the theatre makes an unprecedented advance. And his propensity for the spectacular
side leads him quite logically to ballet. This wealthy
Philistine of mean taste and limited intelligence will guide
to victory the romantic formula of the *ballet blanc*, and even
the idea of an ethereal dance, disregarding the laws of
gravitation, looming vaguely through transparencies. [1]

The cloister of *Robert le Diable* will be the cradle of the
new art. An oral tradition, recorded by Germain
Bapst, which he obtained from M. Ronsin, a distant relative
of Ciceri, acquaints us with the origin of this revolution.
At first, the composer and the poet had wished to stage
the third act of this opera in a fantastic Olympus in
imitation of the classic " devilries " of Gardel's *Psyche*.

---

[1] " Scapin, Frontin and Turcaret added to a glutton, speculator and
sham marquis," such would have been, in the opinion of Philarète
Chasles, the recipe for compounding a Véron. Having undertaken
the management on March 2nd, 1831 (he was then thirty-two), he retired three years later with a profit of 900,000 francs. We shall have
recourse to his *Mémoires*. The scene-painter Séchan declares in his
Mémoires that those of Véron were written by Malitourne, a " ghost "
in the opulent doctor's service.

Duponchel, the advising architect, having learned of this, pointed out to Dr. Véron (who, far from being confident, publicly styled the score as detestable) the insignificance of such a setting, and proposed instead the famous cloister with tombs. Having obtained Meyerbeer's approval, Duponchel dispatched Ciceri to Arles, where he made sketches of Saint-Trophime.[1] At the time of the performance, the nuns, coming forth from their underground dwellings beneath the vaulted arches, fantastically lit by the moon, produced an extraordinary effect. This moonlight, the doctor explains, with legitimate pride, was obtained by means of gas-jets enclosed in boxes hooked to the " flies." It was the first time that gas, already used on the stage itself, was employed in the battens and behind the scenes. The success of the ghoulish nocturne hurt the vanity of the composer, who became of secondary importance.

Of this ballet of the nuns, an invaluable document gives us an idea : Edgar Degas's canvas, dated 1872, which is in the Victoria and Albert Museum, London. In it, before a bored and inattentive audience, may be seen the evolutions of the ladies of the *corps de ballet*, wearing the gauze sleeves of their garments, part monastic robe, part shroud.

Under the great impressionist's brush, the dancers float like a shifting, flaky mass of milky haze. Forms and lines appear broken up, spectral. This *entrée*, devised in 1831 by Coralli (the *maître de ballet* who will arrange *Giselle*), remained the same until forty years later, the eve of the fire in the rue Le Peletier. Not for nothing had the " terrible " Meyerbeer let loose Hell in his score. *Robert le Diable* nearly cost one of its principal interpreters his life. The tenor Nourrit was slightly hurt through a trap giving way beneath his feet. As for Taglioni-Helena, she had a lucky escape. A cloud border fell from the " flies " and would undoubtedly have broken her legs if,

---

[1] Although such is the legend, I have it from M. Louis Schneider, my erudite colleague, that it was not the cloister of Saint-Trophime, but that of Monfort-l'Amaury which served as Ciceri's model.

stretched out on a tombstone, she had not been looking upwards and thus been able to save herself in time. The date, November 21st, 1831, is an important one in the history of dancing. The Infernal Valse of *Robert le Diable* announces the birth of a new style. This novelty will conquer thanks to a masterpiece : *La Sylphide*.

CHAPTER III

THE SYLPHIDE

" Ici Taglioni, la fille des Sylphides,
A fait trembler son aile au bord des eaux perfides."
THÉODORE DE BANVILLE.

Advent of the romantic ballet—A *scenario* by Nourrit—Charles
Nodier in Scotland—*Trilby ou Le Lutin d'Argaïl*—A chore-
grapher's masterpiece—Local colour—Flying dancers—Eugène
Lami and the origin of the *tutu*—The Glory and her headdress.

ON March 12th, 1832, Marie Taglioni created *La
Sylphide*. Alphonse Royer, the genial historian of
the Opéra, justly regards this ballet as the " imperishable
foundation " of her renown. This part is the apex of her
career; it obliterates the trial sketches which were only
preludes to this high attainment. Henceforth, dancer and
character are indivisible. To speak of the Sylphide is to
name Taglioni. At the Opéra she had been a sublime
intruder, foreign to the atmosphere of the place; a gothic
madonna set on an Empire style pedestal. With *La Sylphide*
a new spirit invades the scene, glides over the stage, soars
towards the " flies." No revolution in the order of ideas
could have been more complete. Fairy-tale takes the place
of mythology, and the *ballet blanc* supplants the anacreontic
interlude. Dancing becomes a transcendental language,
charged with spirituality and mystery : a celestial calli-
graphy, it admits nothing profane. The advent of the

new style was greeted with transports of enthusiasm. The first performance of *La Sylphide* is a date to remember, like the publication of the *Harmonies Poétiques*[1] or the triumph of *La Barque de Dante*.[2] Is a similar comparison on a higher plane desired? Théophile Gautier, who was a judge of poetry, looked upon Taglioni as one " of the greatest poets of our age," for him she was " a genius of the same calibre as Lord Byron and Lamartine."

The change of atmosphere and setting in the new piece immediately impresses the musical chronicler of the *Débats*, the same Castil-Blaze who had commented with such reserve on Taglioni's first appearance : " Romanticism lays in ruins the mythology of Homer and Hesiod," he exults. He is right. Great Pan is dead ; the Gods are in exile. The valsing in a ring of elemental spirits has put to flight the goatish race of fauns, and the nocturnal hovering of mournful shades banish henceforth the playful gambols of the Games and the Laughs. Twelve years later, Théophile Gautier will recount in sprightly prose the arrival of the novelty : " After *La Sylphide, Les Filets de Vulcain, Flore et Zéphyre*, were no longer possible : the Opéra was given over to gnomes, undines, salamanders, elves, nixes, wilis, peris—to all that strange and mysterious folk who lend themselves so marvellously to the fantasies of the *maître de ballet*. The twelve palaces in marble and gold of the Olympians were relegated to the dust of storerooms, and the scene-painters received orders only for romantic forests, valleys illumined by the pretty German moonlight reminiscent of Heinrich Heine's ballads. Pink coloured tights always remained pink, because there could be no choregraphy without tights ; only the Greek cothurnus was exchanged for satin shoes. The new style led to a great abuse of white gauze, tulle and tarlatan ; the shades dissolved into mist by means of transparent dresses. White was the only colour used." Thus, in *La Sylphide*, both theme and setting are new. The poetic art of romanticism has permeated the conception ; by what

---

[1] By Lamartine, published 1829—*Tr.*
[2] A painting by Eugène Delacroix—*Tr.*

means has the fashion in literature spread to the ballet, conservative in the highest degree ?

The work is signed by Philippe Taglioni, who arranged the dances for it. There is nothing to show him capable of imagining and writing a theme of this poetic quality. Blaze's review reveals the secret to the public in a witty manner : " The author, who preserves his anonymity, has been brought up (*s'est nourri*) on some good books of Northern mythology. . . ." For " *s'est nourri* " one has only to read " *c'est* Nourrit." This *scenario* is thus a tribute to the admired dancer from the illustrious singer, so soon to sink into melancholy and suicide.

How had they become acquainted ? Two memorable productions had brought the two artists together. First, the appearance of Taglioni, abbess of Sainte-Rosalie, at the head of the chorus of dead nuns, who, in Meyerbeer's *Robert le Diable*, determines the tenor to give himself to the devil. And in *Le Dieu et la Bayadère*, an opera-ballet by Scribe and Auber, Taglioni-Zoloë incites the love of Stranger-Nourrit by virtue of the eloquence of her mute appeal. Together they are drawn up to the sky of Indra in an ingenious swinging contrivance.

Nevertheless, Adolphe Nourrit did not invent the theme of *La Sylphide* himself. We are only indebted to him for the free adaptation to the lyric stage of a work which, ten years earlier, had enjoyed a considerable vogue : the *Trilby* of Charles Nodier, literary forerunner and intermediary, future librarian of the Arsenal, host and moving spirit of the first " *Cénacle*," the club of romantic geniuses. And it is Nourrit again who will adapt from Shakespeare the *scenario* for *La Tempête*, signed by the choreographer Coralli.

Of all the countries where the romantic imagination flits in search of the unusual and the picturesque, Scotland enjoyed the greatest prestige. It was the wild land of the Waverley Novels. Nodier went on a pilgrimage to Sir Walter Scott's domain ; we have an account of this journey ; Nodier also brought back *Trilby ou Le Lutin d'Argail*, *nouvelle écossaise*, a faery idyll racy of the soil and provided

MARIE TAGLIONI IN " LA SYLPHIDE "

From the lithograph by A. E. Chalon

with a gruesome climax. The pure love of Trilby, the malicious elf of the fire-side, and of Jeannie, the pretty ferry-woman of Lake Beau, filled the dreams of the young girls of yesterday. Christmas revues existed only in an embyronic state in the year 1822. Nevertheless, the stage fastened on this literary modernity. Scribe adapted a vaudeville from it for the Gymnase Dramatique ; the Vaudeville replied with a comedy in one act interpolated with songs. The Variétés opposed them with a new variation, and the Panorama Dramatique made fun of the competitors in *Les Trois Trilby*, a folly in one act : all this happened within the space of a single month.

Nourrit's vision retained only the imponderable qualities of Nodier's story, its atmosphere and colour. The " pretty pixy of the cottage, leaping about the edge of scorched stones, with his fiery tartan and smoke-coloured plaid," was not seen at the Opéra. The characters were reversed. James Reuben, a Scottish peasant, is haunted by an intangible being appearing in an aureole of lily-like muslin : the Sylphide, Taglioni.

The theme abounds in graceful situations. And, moreover, " it is not easy to write for legs," as Gautier remarked, who knew all about it.

" My brother, you cannot run with the hare and hunt with the hounds."

This proverb, transposed into verse by Fabre d'Eglantine, a contemporary critic remarks, " has been paraphrased by the author of the theme." These two opposites are reality and imagination, and romantic philosophy favours the latter. James is in love with Effie, the dark peasant girl ; he is loved by the Sylphide, the pale familiar spirit. Which of the two will win him ? James follows the Sylphide into her ethereal kingdom. The witchcraft of a Shakespearean sorceress makes him the murderer of his fragile beloved. Reality takes vengeance on the dreamer in this tragic ending. But the æsthetic of the dream triumphs throughout the performance. *La Sylphide* is the prototype of the romantic ballet. The other poems danced by Taglioni are simply variations of her dual character.

La Fille du Danube merely adds to it some shades of local colour. Gautier will derive inspiration for his *Giselle* from the same situation. Petipa will do the same for his *Bayadère*; ten masterpieces will issue from the same mould.

The maxim for success in 1832 was "to provide frequent opportunities for the appearance of the favourite virtuoso of the public; the piece is written for Mlle. Taglioni; she is the person sought, she is the person awaited." The themes of popular ballads served only as echoes to the sublime elegy of her dancing.

When the curtain rises, the Sylphide is seen on the ſtage, kneeling beside James, who sleeps in an arm-chair; a lithograph from the piƈture by Lepolle, the designer of the coſtumes for *Robert le Diable*, as well as an admirable print by Chalon, demonſtrate the tenderness of that mimed lullaby. The sleeper is awakened by a "kiss from ideal lips"; immediately the vision disappears. The Sylphide appears twice more during the firſt aƈt; sometimes, white and suave, she comes out of the open window, sometimes she comes forth from under the mantelpiece and mingles, invisible, in the betrothal ball and in the highland reel. These episodes are only so-called *pas d'action*, taking part in the mime; we have nothing but drama. The second aƈt, in which the ballet begins, is dominated by the supernatural. Here dancing is supreme. A miſty battalion of sylphides with pink and blue wings appears through the branches of the trees. The daughters of the air hover with timed and rhythmic wings about their siſter. Some attach scarves to the trees and gently swing themselves; others, taking hold of the ends of the branches, bend them down and receive an impetus which carries them into the air. The entrance by fours of the quadrilles, from the back of the ſtage to the front, has remained celebrated in the annals of choregraphic art. In front of the moving screen formed by this *ensemble* begins the *pas de deux* of Taglioni with young Mazilier, an "intelligent and spirited" dancer; it is hunt the shadow, a poetic game of hide and seek, which provides the theme for the duet; now she ſteals away and he pursues her in vain.

Taglioni dances. . . . How does she dance ? " This *pas* is a masterpiece," proclaims Jules Janin in his study for *Les Beautés de l'Opéra*. " No woman dances it, or will dance it, as she danced it." But what does she make of this " almost impossible " part ? " She enters," the same author again tells us, " at once dancing like the Graces and bounding like the Nymphs, with a light and easy step." There are many such statements from which we shall gain little information. She defies criticism and analysis, the defeated critic confesses. Castil-Blaze likewise holds forth on the extraordinary lightness of her dancing, and on the charm of her poses. Rare prints depict her " gliding over flowers without bending them," or discovering a bird's nest in an old oak-tree. But, when words are wanting, the picture usefully takes its place. The iconography of the part is very large. The celebrated coloured lithograph by Achille Devéria depicts the Sylphide, full face, bounding towards the foot-lights with very high *jetés* ; the series by Chalon, a Swiss painter resident in England, display an unusual accuracy of observation, as do also the sketches by the Russian artist, Bassine. A technical analysis of these documents is out of place here. All reveal to us her imponderable flight, emphasised by the floating of some veiling or by further *équilibres sur la pointe* ; under a diaphanous covering is a steel armature ; beneath the frothing of the muslin is a geometrical purity of design. Always the saltatory effort is animated by the slight play of her arms. . . . " I never dreamed of such a wraith ! " exclaimed Charles Nodier.

But Fate is on the watch. The witch's scarf draped over her shoulders causes the Sylphide's wings (" which were useless to her," says a gallant reviewer) to drop off. She dies in the arms of the despairing James. Fabre, the entomologist, would have proved the verisimilitude of this death. Virgin ants have wings which fall off after their love flight. So Nature has foreseen all, even to the endings of ballets. The sylphides cover their sister's face with the scarf and bear her away through the air ; little sylphs uphold her, kissing her feet. This ascension,

47

carried out with the aid of a dozen wires, is a practice dear to producers in the romantic manner. In 1815, Didelot[1] made use of it for the flying ballet in *Flore et Zéphyre*. But, in this dangerous exercise, it was usual for a member of the *corps de ballet* to deputise for the star. This time, Taglioni herself soared towards the borders, between the trees painted by Ciceri.

This risky contrivance did not always work without a hitch. At one performance, two sylphides remained suspended in mid-air ; it was impossible to pull them up or lower them down ; people in the audience cried out in terror ; at last, a machinist risked his life and descended from the roof at the end of a rope to set them free. Some minutes later Mlle. Taglioni, who only spoke this once in all her life (at the theatre, of course) went towards the footlights and said : " Gentlemen, no one has been hurt." Better informed than her contemporary, we could quote at least three speeches by the Sylphide, as terse as this.[2]

The rage for local colour according to the setting of *Rob Roy* or *Montrose* undoubtedly contributed to the " marvellous success " recorded in the newspapers. The very day of the first performance, Furne brought out *Vues Pittoresques d'Ecosse*, engraved by the brothers Johannot. Pierre Ciceri designed the settings. This painter, who, during the Empire, had worked beside Isabey at the designing of models scaled like an architect's plan, achieves a triumph in this new and different style. The scene for the second act, a rocky landscape seen through the trees, was acclaimed a marvel ; it was the Diorama transported to the Opéra ! The lighting effects during the witches' revel entertained and delighted : illumination by gas had lost nothing of its novelty ; if they no longer played before candles at the Comédie Française, they still had only oil lamps there. Another artist intimately associated with the legend of the Sylphide is Eugène Lami, a pupil of Baron Gros, whose gouaches and vignettes evoke the pomp of

---

[1] Didelot made use of two dancers only ; Taglioni had twelve.

[2] Charles Maurice asserts that, at this same performance, Taglioni " fell down very clumsily," an incident which this arrant liar relates with joy.

48

the July monarchy. He had already designed for the Opéra the costumes for *La Tentation* ; in dressing Taglioni he settled the correct dress for the romantic ballet. Lami cut down the " gown that makes the monk," as the French proverb goes.

In imitation of the tragedian Talma, Gardel had introduced during the Empire the same reform that David had introduced into painting. The dancers put on the Greek tunic, whose pleats draped the body and followed its lines. Eugène Lami invented the *tutu,* as it is usually termed, a kind of muslin underwear which puffs out the dress of white crêpe. This costume, the shape of a bell or inverted corolla, enables the dancer to *dégager* with ease ; it is adapted for springing and running. At the same time, this ingenious cloud of gauze radiates an idea of pure poetry. No ornament oppresses it, scarcely a posy modestly conceals the hollow of the breasts. A garland of flowers placed on the hair, a triple row of pearls around the neck, bracelets to match, a narrow sky-blue ribbon encircling the wasp waist—these complete the seraphic winged silhouette.

We have erred in forgetting one man, associated moreover with *La Sylphide*—Schneitzhoeffer, called Chênecerf, professor at the Conservatoire, who, to employ a pretty solecism of the period, had " musicked " the ballet. Castil-Blaze doted on the excellent music by Schneitzhoeffer, the man with the Balzacian name, and extolled it as " infinitely remarkable." Gautier affirmed that this ballet-music was among the best in existence. By itself, the composer's name, bristling with consonants, was one destined to be forgotten.[1] Shall we attack this glory already so old-fashioned ? What does it matter whether he borrowed his sorcerer's theme from Paganini ? His melodies were able to inspire Taglioni !

A thousand little things convey much better than banal praises the impression produced by the work and the chief

[1] The composer, a facetious person and fond of mystifications, resigned himself with a smile to this strange misfortune. He put on his visiting cards this satirical phrase : Schneitzhoeffer (pronounced Bertrand).

49

aĉtor. Blaze had juŝt launched the verb "*taglioniser*"; Janin used "*sylphide*" as an adjeĉtive. A ŝtill greater proof of renown, Marie Taglioni influences head-dress even.[1] The Maison Beauvais creates a "*turban Sylphide*." In the auŝtere *Vie de Rancé* written by Chateaubriand in his seventieth year, there is tender mention of " Mlle. Taglioni's ethereal dances." Victor Hugo fashions a madrigal for her and dedicates a book to her in these terms : *A vos pieds, à vos ailes.* But these auguŝt tokens of respeĉt are not so convincing to the hiŝtorian as certain portraits by Grèvedon, which depiĉt the Parisienne of 1832 with her hair dressed " *à la Sylphide*."

[1] " In imitation of Marie Taglioni, who then exercised a considerable influence," we learn from Louis Maigron in his work *Romantisme et la Mode*, " all kinds of frills were introduced into dresses and bodices to make them rustling and billowy : berthas, aprons, lace, scarves, pale veilings—all these were used to give woman a seraphic and ideal appearance."

MARIE TAGLIONI IN " LA SYLPHIDE "
From the lithograph by Achille Devéria
after the statuette by Barre

CHAPTER IV

THE APOGEE

" Adam t'ouvrit un nouveau monde,
Un palais de cristal sous l'onde,
Sylphide de l'air et des eaux."
MÉRY.

The day after the victory—The plagiarisms of Philippe Taglioni—*La Révolte des Femmes*—*Le Bain Turc*—Military ballet—The failure of *Brézilia*—Taglioni and Vestris—A ghost—*La Fille du Danube*—Jacob's ladder—A print by Gavarni.

HENCEFORTH, Taglioni's identity is, as it were, abolished. She is mingled with the image of the Sylphide which becomes her " aſtral body." She will create many other parts. But none of these successive charaĉters will supplant that supreme incarnation of her being, with one exception, perhaps, that of *La Fille du Danube*, in 1836 ; but we shall see that this ballet is mainly a variation on the original theme, fashioned out of the same spiritual matter as the *Sylphide*. However, many other parts will follow one another, significant episodes, during those four years in which Taglioni's vocation culminates. These are true landmarks in her career, diſturbed at this time by a marriage in which she found no happiness. We shall recount in its proper place the ſtory of her conjugal misfortunes ; we muſt say from the very firſt that true affeĉtion did not founder with this shipwreck and that her son was deſtined to be present to close her eyes for the laſt time. In the meanwhile, the dancer's private life does not arouse the benevolent or malicious curiosity of the public, except in so far as it concerns her theatrical success. She is the spoilt darling of the stalls, the prisoner of her own success.

Immediately on the reopening, Philippe Taglioni sought to consolidate the triumph of *La Sylphide*, in which he had shared, by producing a new work. Purveyor by appointment to his daughter, he becomes a permanency at the Opéra ; but Marie's incomparable prestige does not always spare him from the scoffs of the critics. Thus, their sardonic remarks hail on *Nathalie, Laitière Suisse,* which met with a *succés d'estime* on November 7th, 1832. The music was written by Girovetz and Carafa, feeble disciples of Rossini ; the theme was signed by the choregrapher. This incoherent and insipid plot must have been suggested by the famous " *Tyrolienne* " in *Guillaume Tell,* which he tried to fill out by means of some action of his own concoction, in which the confusion of a dummy figure with living people creates imbroglios supposed to be amusing.[1] Again, Eugène Lami dressed the Sylphide, whose silhouette he had already established, as an Alpine shepherdess. Whatever the stupidity of the plot, Marie Taglioni's name charmed the crowd ; *La Laitière Suisse* attained forty-eight performances and died a natural death. It was quite different with *Brézilia* which fell flat on the first night and dragged wearily on for five performances. The echo of this failure is found in one of Balzac's studies of women. But we must not anticipate events, the most famous of which will be the creation of *La Révolte au Sérail,* ballet in three acts ; the music is by Théodore Labarre, the " words," according to the poster, are by Taglioni.

Since *La Sylphide,* Marie had no more faithful minstrel than the author of *L'Ane Mort et la Femme Assassinée* ;[2]

[1] " The ballet *Nathalie* belongs to the foolish type," declares Gautier, at the time of the revival in 1837 ; " it is full of Swiss chalets, as might be guessed."

[2] Jules Janin.

he did not tire of devising for her the most extravagant epithets and eked out his material with the most tedious repetition. But to sharpen his keen pen he seized upon our Philippe, whom he made his butt. In his notice of *La Révolte au Sérail*, he devoted himself to this to his heart's content.

"There are some who declare," he begins insidiously, "that it is necessary to have an idea in order to devise a ballet; they are mistaken. This good M. Taglioni proves it. He is quite the most artless of men in general and of choregraphers in particular, it is impossible to be less of a poet. . . . It would be one of the most beautiful sights in the world to see M. Taglioni composing a poem and above all to see him *writing* one with his pen. . . . His theme is merely a vague excuse to bring together a number of dancers, many ribbons, much lace, many turbans, and many bare shoulders." Not content with having humiliated the author, he accuses the unlucky choregrapher of plagiarism. The sister of Henri, a *maître de ballet* who had his hour of fame, had complained to the critic about the thefts of Taglioni, who, having no ideas of his own, took them from everyone else. The dances in *La Révolte au Sérail* were no more his than those in *La Sylphide*.

What is the foundation for this accusation? Provoked by jealousy of a rival, it is no less plausible. However, *maîtres de ballet* throughout the ages have complained of similar pilferings. Their work is, so to speak, collective; all new *pas*, all "difficulties" happily vanquished become public property; *res nullius*, they are incorporated in the living tradition. It is just the same with themes; once an idea has succeeded, it is continually repeated; the titles, names and properties alone are changed. So J. J. did not delay to insist upon this accusation. "M. Taglioni," he concludes with a smile, "is the greatest choregrapher in the world; he has his daughter—Mlle. Taglioni—whom he took from no one." And, having said this, how can one be angry with him?

As a matter of fact, this is saying a good deal. To understand and minister to so great a personality, to suit the vocabulary of the language of the dance to her style and abilities, to accord her the right impetus for her airy spring, was no mean occupation. As for the theme selected, it is neither less worthy nor more conventional than any other ballet theme. Granted that its orientalism is excessively artificial; but an oriental evocation steeped in ethnological accuracy would make the mimed action—interrupted with stylised and abstract dances—incomprehensible. When you are talking of ballet you must renounce probability to arrive at the quite different logic of figured movement danced to music. But, if *La Sylphide* was full of intimate lyricism and conventional picturesque, *La Révolte* delighted by a purely visual splendour.

To evoke Granada under the Moorish dominion, Ciceri collaborated with two of the members of a team soon to be renowned, Feuchère and Despléchins. It was they who painted the scene for the Court of the Lions at the Alhambra, which is the setting for the prologue. We see that Zulma, the favourite sultana of Mahomet, King of Granada, burns with passion for Ismail, a victorious warrior, acted by Perrot.

There, certainly, is a situation which calls for a *pas de deux*; the spectator gladly forgets the drama to see them dance. Jules Janin's description of this affords us but a feeble picture of it. He ignores technical terms and his prose has nothing of the plasticity of expression which enables Gautier, master of the *mot juste*, to fashion his phrases. Janin, a frivolous author, flounders in vagueness; we have to follow him, while he vainly seeks to emphasise the novelty of the *pas de deux*. " Yesterday, she came to us *sur la pointe*, or else she balanced from side to side, throwing her body sometimes to right and sometimes to left; at the moment she throws herself backwards . . ." What does the reader make of this brief outline? The second act opens with a new and charming picture, the bathing-pool of the sultan's wives who plunge into a white marble basin; eight dancers raise their heads, taxing all their ingenuity not to reveal more than the most minute area of bare shoulder. This modest counterpart of Ingres's

Bain Turc was for our great-grandfathers the equivalent of the bathing-pool at the Casino de Paris ! The first odalisque to emerge from the water is Zulma. The sultana's toilet proceeds to the sound of music, when a slave presents her with a magic posy. This talisman changes to a sheaf of spears ; the odalisques seize upon them, when, warned by the eunuch Misouf, who is the clown of the piece, the enraged sultan appears. But the spears turn to lyres and the conspirators are saved. With Mahomet's departure there is a new transformation ; the rebels take the field. The last act transports us to the camp in the Alpuxarras. Zulma reviews her large army, for which even the Old Guard of the quadrilles has been mobilised and of whom Mlle. Brocard, a veteran of the dance, celebrated for her unchangeable beauty, is the Cambronne. If we can credit the descriptions recorded, there was nothing prettier than these military evolutions ; the *corps de ballet* executed them as one man ; their slender legs, revealed by turned-back dresses, moved with martial grace. Their uniforms were designed by the architect Duponchel, Dr. Véron's future successor to the management of the Opéra. After many theatrical effects, the protective genius reunited Ismail and Zulma in a final apotheosis, and Mlle. Taglioni, acclaimed with fervour, reappeared to take her call, " the amiable, modest, and reserved woman " having resigned the arrogance of the fierce sultana.

Taglioni took no part in the final performance of *Ali Baba*, a story from *The Thousand and One Nights*, on which Scribe had based an absurd opera : but she was called upon to save the piece from complete failure ; this last resource was the more effective in that Taglioni was seen to perform the very *entrechats* and *pas battus* which she was supposed to have banished for ever. She also gave splendour to a final revival of Spontini's *La Vestale*.

Now comes a very significant, if not decisive, episode in the dancer's life, to which it will be proper to devote the whole of the next chapter. It concerns the rivalry between Taglioni and Fanny Elssler, engaged by Véron more to reduce the pride of the overbearing Sylphide than to replace her during her pretended illnesses. It can be said that this epic struggle lay heavy on the whole careers of these two dancers ; not only did public opinion compare them, but their own acts and gestures were, for some ten years, dominated by this contest. Stroke and counter-stroke were ruled by an implacable and persevering strategy. This great quarrel cast a shadow over their two lives ; we shall examine it in all its phases ; in the meantime this mention must suffice. As formerly, the Opéra posters only serve as landmarks in these annals of theatrical glory. On August 8th, 1835, we again find Taglioni dancing at her benefit (which produces 25,000 francs for the Sylphide) a new ballet made up by her father, a work which has all the appearance of nonsense ; I have already mentioned *Brézilia, ou La Tribu des Femmes,* for which Gallembourg composed the tedious music.

In some far away kingdom of Florida, amidst palm-trees painted by Philastre and Cambon, struts a race of amazons who have sworn eternal hatred towards men. Zamore falls into their hands ; he would flee if Brezilia's beauty had not captivated him. The law of the land demands his punishment. Who will be his jailer until dawn ? The most feared amazon, she who leaps the highest and whose arrow speeds the farthest. In this athletic struggle Taglioni wins. She aids the prisoner to escape, and, after a choregraphic combat, the lovers win their suit. This theme, beloved of folklore, by Greek myths no less than Breton legends, will still provide for many ballets of the type of *Nisida* or Delibes' *Sylvia.* Nevertheless, rhythmic combats, in which survives the memory of those military ballets which were the pyrrhic of the ancients or the parade step of the *grand siècle,* are perpetuated in ballet after ballet ; it is one of the great themes of the *danse d'ensemble* which tradition has preserved by transforming them.

Moreover, in succession to this feeble work, Taglioni contrived a memorable surprise for her admirers. She appeared in a *Menuet de Cour,* an adorable *pasticcio,* by giving her hand to Auguste Vestris. To see her—in full dress, demi-paniers and powdered hair—thus bring the past back

MARIE TAGLIONI IN "LA FILLE DU DANUBE"
From a lithograph

to life produced the greatest emotion. And she not only had the dress, but the deportment, gesture and look ; all were astonished to see the ethereal, phantom-like Sylphide " no less at ease on earth than in the air."

Vestris appeared, all gold embroidery, with leg straight, to receive his share of the applause and flowers. At that moment he was seventy-five, sixty-three years separated him from his first appearance ; he retired from the Opéra in 1816. Taglioni's gracious act in reconciling romanticism with the rococo seemed to prove the continuity of the traditional school and the vitality of the species. She did more by inviting her rival to take part in the festival. The sisters Elssler appeared in a new *pas de deux*, " Fanny always in the arms of Thérèse who protects her, supports her, lifts her to admiration. Two Germans of such fine quality ! " exclaims Janin, and his concealed ill-humour comes to light in this displeasing peroration. The critic, whose notices are for us the most abundant source of information, announces a month later the farewell of " Her Airiness, Mlle. Taglioni," and, inexhaustible, persists in telling us that " she has been ethereal and artless, white and chaste."

Next year we shall find him back at his post to praise that *Fille du Danube* which sums up Taglioni's style for the last time and brings the creative period of her professional career to an end.

" This is the very poetic sequel to *La Sylphide*," the critic of the *Débats* can justly remark, " the two conceptions are analogous, with the shade of difference that the supernatural resides no longer in the ether but in the depths of the waters." What does it matter, since " all elements are permitted to Mlle. Taglioni except the earth, and she walks on the waves as she soars in the air." Of all the elemental spirits which haunt German folklore, the nixie or water-elf, which lives at the bottom of a well, is the most familiar to the imagination of story-tellers. The brothers Grimm, those Perraults of Germany, as well as Hans Christian Andersen, the Swabian poet Moerike, de la Motte-Fouqué, the German romanticist of French origin—have all been captivated by the charming amphibious vampire, Homer's siren became the golden-haired Loreley of Heinrich Heine's ballads.

The action of Adolphe Adam's ballet takes place at Donaueschingen, a real place on the map, the time is the half-legendary, half-historic middle ages. It is the culmination of the peasant idyll and the castellated style, that imitation, flamboyant gothic which inspired Celestin Nanteuil's frontispieces and which Gustave Doré carried to excess; in short, everything is there—the thatched cottage and turreted keep.

The theme, signed Philippe and devised in an inimitably strained and affected style, falls into two parts; one relates the tradition on which the ballet is founded, the other gives what we should term the scenes of the play expressed in terms of the dance.

For this occasion, the Sylphide is baptised Fleur-des-Champs[1], or Feldblume, which, in German, means the same thing; of mysterious origin, she was found in the grass of a river-bank by parents who brought her up. She is sixteen (the dancer had only to halve her age to arrive at the exact figure) and dancing is her whole life. Rudolph, Baron Willibald's page, is of the same opinion. Having danced until they can do no more, they sleep beneath a tree, like Daphnis and Chloë. The nymph of the Danube places the mysterious bethrothal ring on their fingers and " marries the perfume of their breaths." But their happiness is already threatened. Heralds invite the villagers to an entertainment given by the Baron. Willibald, for complicated and sinister reasons, vows eternal hatred against any woman of high lineage. He desires to marry a woman of the people. His ball is only a competition of beauty and dancing of which he is an obviously partial judge. Baronesses and serfs compete in grace, and soon flowers win the victory over diamonds; and the gauze of light skirts triumph over the satin of court dresses. Now, Willibald chooses Fleur-des-Champs. She repulses him. The baron implores her, then threatens her. She throws

[1] Flower of the Fields—*Tr.*

herself into the Danube. The passionate drama is solved in the actual theme ; the mystic dawn of the *ballet blanc* begins to break for the victim, mystery is superimposed on comic opera. In such a setting we find once more the essential principle of romantic ballet begun by the librettist of the *Sylphide*. The sentimental struggle of the first act hastens to pass to the picturesque, highly coloured, national dances ; among the flashing costumes gleam Scottish tartans or slashed trunks, caps with eagle's feathers or damascened morions. The action, primed by the lovers, grows more violent to its conclusion.

In the second act, the disembodied persons, colourless, wearing the white uniform of pure ideas, express themselves only in the secret tongue of classical ballet. Nothing is altered in *La Fille du Danube*. The poetry of the type requires, moreover, an interlude which connects the two ideas ; the supernatural revealing itself to the crude earthly intelligence by means of signs and apparitions. Hence the spirit of Fleur-des-Champs appears to Rudolph ; it is the Jacob's ladder erected between the two acts ; vainly does the page seek to grasp the smiling phantom ; in desperation, he too throws himself into the Danube.

At the bottom of the river, he falls into a large *ballabile* of veiled nymphs, among whom he recognises his beloved. Having passed this test, he returns to the surface bearing his sweet prey with him.

The success was overwhelming ; within a fortnight the *galop* of the first act invaded every ballroom ; the dances were considered to be very artistically composed, and d'Orchevillers' costumes to be smart ; Mazilier-Rudolph was thought to be too slender and too short of breath. " It must be a terrible trial to follow that woman who flies like the wind."

And Taglioni ? Once more her dancing is described for us in such general terms that, at most, it can only convey to us the critic's emotion. " In turn, heroine and phantom, so ethereal and so sad, so passionate and so calm, she executed," asserts Janin, " with the most natural air the most wonderful *tours de force* in dancing that this world has ever seen." What are these unheard-of difficulties ? The critic evades the question by confessing that his pen is vanquished by that indefatigable feather. A charming picture comes to fill this gap—an engraving after Gavarni, who appears to have designed the model for Fleur-des-Champs's costume. The artist to the *Mode* draws one of the most pleasing silhouettes of Taglioni. Her costume is more scanty than that for the Sylphide. The low bodice, leaving the shoulders free, is without ornament ; only a posy adorns the gauze skirt ; a garland is placed on the braided hair. But in this portrait sketched by Gavarni under the pretext of cutting out a pattern, there is a fullness of contour like a maturity of form which alters nothing in its touching purity. No other print shows us Taglioni in that flowering of the " woman of thirty," the supreme growth which precedes decline.

The Sylphide's new incarnation made a furore. Once more fashion, a delicate seismograph, registered the shock ; taffetas the colour of the waves of the Danube became all the rage. It is the nature of dancing to push frivolity to its utmost limit. Stendhal tells us that when the beautiful Marie Medina, the wife of the choreographer Vigano, became *enceinte*, the exquisites of Vienna wore little false stomachs *à la Vigano*.

CHAPTER V

A CHOREGRAPHIC DUEL

" Enfin va se juger l'importante querelle
Qui divise le monde et le tient en suspens."

J. BERCHOUX.

Fanny Elssler and her Plutarch—" Parallel lives "—Fanny's first appearances—Her struggle with Taglioni—Gautier's *volte face*—The Sylphide's victory—The *Cachucha* and the *pas* from *La Gitane*.

AUGUSTE EHRHARD'S book on Fanny Elssler[1] affords us, quite rightly, the most detailed biography of Marie Taglioni. At one part of his story the Sylphide's " Plutarch " also feels himself imperiously forced to adopt the method of " parallel lives." Every author who is full of his subject is naturally inclined to champion the personage whom, with full knowledge of the facts, he has chosen from among all others. Without wishing to fall into that pardonable error, or to resurrect a quarrel which has been laid to rest for many generations, we firmly believe ourselves to be on the right side. Fanny owes the greater part of her renown to her rivalry with Taglioni ; she elevated herself by crossing swords with that seraphic genius. Not that her attainments were not brilliant. Her assets are precious ; she embodies an essential aspect of the romantic ideal—all its colour, sensual ardour, personality. The opposite of Taglioni, she filled a void. Neither of them can compass the whole gamut of their profession. Fanny was Liszt's

[1] *Une Vie de Danseuse. Fanny Elssler.* (Plon.) 1909.

61

Rhapsody coming after a slow valse of Chopin. I shall not say that she is the shadow of that light, because Taglioni is a dreamy or mournful shadow, while Elssler frolics in the sunlight.

However it may be, this women's war moved all Paris, just as had done in former days the joust between Sallé and Camargo, and the famous quarrel between the Gluckists and the Piccinists, and also, at the period we are discussing, the competition between the singers Duprez and Nourrit, who sealed his imagined defeat with his blood. This conflict was the more difficult in that each dancer in turn wished to trespass on the other's territory. Fanny attempted to spread the Sylphide's wings, while Taglioni, in spite, seized on the castanets of the "Andalusian from the North."

Text in hand, M. Ehrhard indites in his charming book, so full of information and so well written, the story of that epic struggle ; it is only the purely choregraphic viewpoint of the subject that escapes him, or which has no interest for him. He dwells willingly on a testimony as magnificently eloquent as it is passionately biased ; that of Théophile Gautier. Without deliberately transgressing justice, but not without ill humour against the rival, the poet pleads the cause of the preferred artist and also of the woman he admires. He bows, in spite of all, before Taglioni, but he devotes himself to Elssler. In weighing the two styles he cannot help tilting the scale. It is true that none of Taglioni's followers spoke of her with a more consummate art than that adversary. We can state that public opinion was on the side of the Taglionists. But to celebrate her victory she had only the insipid verbosity of Jules Janin. Thus her praise is written in sand; Fanny Elssler's features are engraved on marble with a golden stylus.

Born at Vienna on June 23rd, 1810, Fanny Elssler was the god-daughter of the illustrious Joseph Haydn, to whom her father filled the post of house-steward. The French choregrapher, Aumer, initiated her into the mysteries of the art ; Barbaja, Rossini's famous impresario, got her to dance in Italy. A liaison with the Chevalier Friedrich von Gentz,

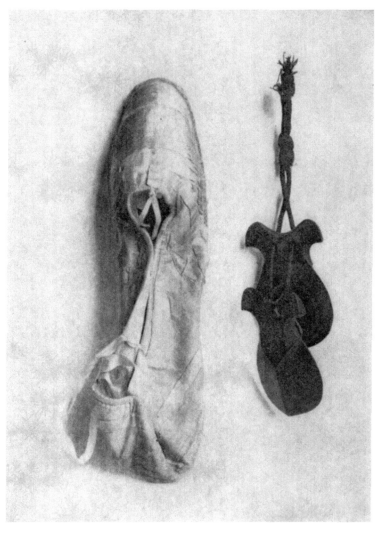

SOME SOUVENIRS OF MARIE TAGLIONI
A ballet shoe worn by the famous dancer, also the castanets used by her in
" La Gitane "
(*Musée de l'Opéra*)

an old beau of the Congress at Vienna, a diplomat and dilettante, occupied two years of her life. This is the Gentz whom Rostand, in his *L'Aiglon*, makes the easily deceived spy and vile tool of Metternich. That is merely an "*image d'Epinal*" slandering this scholarly nobleman. The old dandy taught the little plebeian the ways of the world and developed her intelligence. Rostand's play repeated another legend, that of which the Duc de Reich-stadt is the hero. This story, launched by Charles Maurice, backed by Janin, and immediately denied, was too intriguing not to be on everyone's lips. Dazzling successes won at Berlin inaugurate the wandering life of the young Viennese. At London, Dr. Véron will seek her out; besides, she is living there in a modest fashion then. He engages both her and her elder—and taller—sister, Thérèse, at a salary of 40,000 francs per annum; deliberately, the ingrate will set her up in opposition to Taglioni.

What end had he in mind in thus dividing the sovereignty of dancing? Did he wish, by the employment of such menaces, to break down the capriciousness of Taglioni, a tyrannical and sovereignly fantastic star? Or was it merely his intention to make up in this manner for the *diva's* frequent absences? However it may be, he surrounded Fanny's first appearances with an unusual pomp and heralded them with a well-conducted press campaign. Fanny Elssler appeared in *La Tempête*, an indigestible adaptation from Shakespeare's fairy play, on September 15th, 1834. The ballet seems dull to the public. But Fanny begins the fairy Alcine's *variation* and the wind of success blows in gusts! Taglioni, smiling, applauds; the crowd, like a big child, turns towards her box to see what effect this triumph of the rival produces on her; Véron must have rubbed his hands with joy. He fostered this rivalry and did everything to add fuel to it. Even before that evening, semi-official bulletins sowed discord. A paragraph in the *Courrier des Théâtres*, the organ of that parasite Charles Maurice, declared that the *corps de ballet*, vanquished by the graces displayed by the pretty German at rehearsals, plumed themselves on being Elsslerists, as formerly they

had been enthusiastic Taglionists. Besides, the appointed
flatterer drew a seductive image of the new-comer, not
lacking in technical details. He saw in her a great vivacity,
an astonishing vigour, an abundance of well-beaten *entrechats* (and Taglioni rarely performed beaten steps), strong
pointes, legs which moved softly even when higher than
the hips, which proved her to be " well placed," and
talked incessantly about her beauty. This venal, but
clear-sighted, unprincipled fellow, carrying the discussion
on gymnastic territory, plainly defines the difference
between the two styles. Others, such as the excellent
Charles de Boigne in his *Petits Mémoires de l'Opéra*, merely
enlarge on the competent opinion formulated by Charles
Maurice.

" Artistic people," writes the latter, the day following
Fanny's first appearance, " call this style of dancing
taqueté, to explain that it consists mainly of quick, little
steps, precise, close together, digging into the stage . . .
the *pointes* play a great part in it. . . . It was impossible
to find a more striking contrast to the talent . . . of Mlle.
Taglioni, whose dancing is altogether *ballonné*." This is
what was said. And those who spread about Paris this
pun : " Is it a woman or *est-ce l'air*," missed the whole
point. Because Fanny, a *terre à terre* dancer, had nothing
to seek in the heavens where Marie soared, a dancer of
elevation.

The distinction must not be regarded as purely formal,
it corresponds to the profound dualism of dancing ; it is
no more a question of doing, but a manner of being.

Taqueté is the intoxication of living on earth. *Ballonné*
is the desire to reach the skies. In one case there is a
quickly scanned *staccato* of *pointes* which rebound, " like
golden arrows on a marble pavement," to a jerky rhythm
of strings plucked in 2-4 time. In the other, there is the
legato of great *paraboli* described in the air to a waltz movement, or the slow advancing of *développés* in adagio, sustained
by the singing of the bow. The *terre à terre* dancer rejoices
in executing a *pas* ; the dancer of *élévation* is transfigured !
In mime, each of these temperaments employs a different

medium of expression. The " terrestial " relies on dramatic and direct gesture ; her actions express with vivacity the sentiments which animate her. The elegiac chooses the symbolic and abstract language of dance steps ; with her body she traces hieroglyphics, legible signs made indelible through her emotion. We must confess a preference for the sibyl to the bacchante crowned with vine-leaves. The head of the " plastic school " judges otherwise. On the occasion of the first appearances of Mlle. Fitz-James, the skeleton dancer, " thin as a lizard, transparent as the horn pane of a lantern," Théophile Gautier gives a cut-and-dried definition of dancing (in the issue of November 27th, 1837) which permits of no equivocation.

" Dancing consists of nothing more than the art of displaying elegant and precise shapes in different positions favourable to the development of lines. . . . It is essentially pagan, materialistic and sensual." We see that this profession of faith attacks, through the inconsistent and lamentable transparency of poor Fitz-James, the very muse of spiritual dancing—Marie Taglioni. At this moment, Elssler prepares to strike a great blow. She actually lays hands on the Sylphide's crown ; this attempt is hazardous in the extreme. No more does the pretty usurper ask genuine praise from her critic, but a justification in full. He copes with the cry of sacrilege from the Taglionists and affirms, though not without a visible trace of embarrassment, that the pre-eminence of Taglioni as compared with Elssler might quite well be contested ; he is seen to be perplexed on being confronted with this matter of delicate conscience ; but he resumes his mastery of his resources in the dual and antithetic portrait he draws of the two rivals.

" Mlle. Fanny Elssler . . . is the dancer for men as Mlle. Taglioni was[1] the dancer for women, she has elegance, beauty, a bold and petulant vigour, a sparkling smile and, above all, an air of Spanish vivacity tempered

[1] I draw the reader's attention to this insidious preterite ; it relegates to the *past* the triumphs of Taglioni who is only absent.

E

by her German artlessness. . . . When Fanny dances, one
thinks of a thousand pleasant things . . ." and the journalist
allows his imagination to wander about the metopes of
the Parthenon and on the terraces of Syracuse.

"Mlle. Taglioni," he continues, "reminded you of cool
and shaded valleys where a white vision suddenly emerges
from the bark of an oak to greet the eyes of a young,
surprised and blushing shepherd, she resembled unmistak-
ably those fairies of Scotland, of whom Walter Scott
speaks, who roam in the moonlight near the mysterious
fountain, with a necklace of dew-drops and a golden
thread for girdle.

"If one may make use of the expression, Mlle. Taglioni
is a Christian dancer, Mlle. Fanny Elssler is a pagan dancer.
The daughters of Miletus, beautiful Ionians, so celebrated
in antiquity, must have danced in the same manner," he
concludes ; and so great is his enthusiasm that he surrep-
titiously inserts in his prose an Alexandrine worthy of
André Chenier.

However, we can find only one critic who rallied to the
Austrian's aid ; the chronicler of the *Nouvelliste*, Barbey
d'Aurevilly. The so-called "*connétable* of letters" delights
in the "audacities of Fanny Elssler, who effaced completely the idolatrous memories of that pair of compasses,
composed of little flesh and much bone, called Mlle.
Taglioni." Having charged the enemy full tilt in his
criticism, the dandy confesses in his private diary that
which Théo kept to himself : "I love Fanny to the point
of telling lies for her . . . so I have slaughtered Taglioni
on her altar."

However, the matter was judged on appeal ; Charles
Maurice having declared that the "revival of *La Sylphide*
had been a mistake on the part of a very gifted dancer,"
the public were of his opinion. In proof of his words,
the public let Fanny dance to empty houses. But she was
obstinate and faced the rising storm. Having annexed
La Sylphide, she then laid hands on *La Fille du Danube*.
This resulted in an unprecedented scandal. Exceeding
their instructions, the hired applauders commanded by

M. Auguste, the illustrious chief of the *claque* (immortalised by Balzac under the name of Braulard), ill-treated the Taglionists, who had taken it upon themselves to hiss. Théophile Gautier, putting a good face on matters, fought against the fiasco by reiterating his argument. He did not hesitate to connect this disagreeable event with glorious memories of the past :

" There was a tumult, riot, bacchanale, exchange of blows, frenzied bravos, fiendish whistles ; just as in the days of the finest classical and romantic duels, so that one might have imagined oneself at a performance of *Le More de Venise* or of *Hernani.*" The comparison is dubious ; it was no more a case of youthful rebels furnished with red tickets bearing the Castilian device *hierro* who led the fight, but the gallery *claque* appointed to down intriguers. No longer does the critic seek to remain fair ; he becomes aggressive : " To our mind, Mlle. Elssler is quite the equal of Mlle. Taglioni. . . . Besides, she possesses what Mlle. Taglioni lacks, a profound sense of drama ; she dances as well as her rival and mimes better." Impelled by passion, he concludes by attacking his adversary at her weakest point.

" First, she (Fanny) has an immense advantage in that she is prettier and younger." There is the tender spot, the very mention of which excites quarrels between stars. The blossoming of a dancer is limited to a few brief days ; the supreme display of her muscular faculties is restricted to some ten years ; every day of existence shortens this reprieve. Elssler, like Taglioni, will survive her retirement more than thirty years ; but there is a difference of six years between them to which Théophile Gautier alludes. In 1844, Fanny will have attained Marie's age in 1838 ; at that moment, Elssler's altogether devoted journalist and faithful correspondent will find Taglioni younger than ever and will be unable to say a word of remembrance for the other. But we are anticipating events.

When, in July, 1840, Taglioni returned to Paris, Fanny was in America and Théo was travelling in Spain. In her turn the Sylphide retook possession of her domain and made an adroit raid into her enemy's territory. And then we see the anonymous critic of the *Revue des Deux Mondes* avenge her for all the outrages she had suffered, by giving no quarter. He completely reverses the comparison set up by Gautier, and this time Fanny is unlucky enough to be away.

When he discusses Taglioni, the critic seems to model his style on the sermons of Père Lacordaire ; an enthusiasm amounting to worship pervades his unctuous prose : " The other week, a wave of good luck swept through the auditorium of the Opéra. . . . Taglioni feels that it is her masterpiece (we are referring to *La Sylphide*). Thus she treats it with reverence as she changes the details, adding here and there scenes and episodes which round off the action and afford excuse for steps in which her talent finds a means of displaying itself in a new light ! " If we can believe the author of the article, who takes effect for cause, Taglioni was guided by instinct alone ; she danced as a bird sings ; the others, all of them, are only worthy executants :

" Everywhere one is conscious of effort and labour, Mlle. Elssler perfects her gestures and prepares at leisure her most insignificant pose. Mlle. Noblet had to make two attempts before launching herself in an adventurous pirouette. The art of other dancers is learned like a trade, that of Mlle. Taglioni springs from nature."

Having stated this heresy, for nothing is more specious than his reasoning, the critic " springs like a lion " on Fanny and rends her to pieces. " And to say after that, that others besides Taglioni have wished to dance *La Sylphide* ! In place of Mlle. Taglioni, put Mlle. Elssler ; the ballet is possible no longer. With the best will in the world, one cannot but admit that that beautiful girl, whose steps made so much noise, would be invisible as Effie." We know already from Théophile Gautier that the *terre à terre* dancer had had to alter all the steps of the part, as they were too high-pitched, as we should say of a singer, for her diapason. But Taglioni does not stop at this revenge. " How well was Taglioni avenged for

Mlle. Elssler's petty usurpations. For she took everything
from her, even to her *Cachucha* ! "

To realise the importance of these words it is necessary
to explain that the *Cachucha* is the brightest jewel in that
" cardboard crown." It was Taglioni once more who,
with her *Tyrolienne*, had introduced the charming practice
of these stylisations of popular dances of different provinces ;
the period was smitten with that European exoticism come
to animate the austere monotony of the traditional school.
The *Cachucha* was one of these " artistic transpositions "
of the frisky *Boleros* which Dolorès Serral, the Andalusian,
had revealed at the Opéra balls. A great noise of castanets
replied to the call on Hernani's horn. Soon, so far as
ballet went, there were no more Pyrenees. Théo's study
in *Les Beautés de l'Opéra* affords us more than a mere idea
of what Fanny's *Cachucha* was like : he conveys its
picturesque, sensuous sparkle :

" She comes forward in her pink satin *basquine* trimmed
with wide flounces of black lace ; her skirt, weighted at
the hem, fits tightly over her hips ; her slender waist
boldly arches and causes the diamond ornament on her
bodice to glitter ; her leg, smooth as marble, gleams
through the frail mesh of her silk stocking ; and her
little foot, at rest, seems but to await the signal of the
music. How charming she is with her big comb, the rose
behind her ear, her lustrous eyes and her sparkling smile !
At the tips of her rosy fingers quiver ebony castanets.
Now she darts forward ; the castanets begin their sonorous
chatter. With her hands she seems to shake down great
clusters of rhythm. How she twists ! How she bends !
What fire ! What voluptuousness ! What precision !
Her swooning arms toss about her drooping head, her
body curves backwards, her white shoulders almost graze
the ground. What a charming posture ! Would you not
say that in that hand which seems to skim the dazzling
barrier of the footlights she gathers up all the desires and
all the enthusiasm of the spectators ? "

Although censurious tongues wagged, the *Cachucha*
gained universal approval. Barre's statuette records, quite

69

as well as Devéria's print, Fanny's famed movement of the hips. Now the *pas* in *La Gitane* (the ballet requested from Auber as a set-off to the *Gypsy* created by Elssler), which Taglioni danced for her farewell performances amid a rain of bouquets, is simply the *Cachucha* stripped of everything brutal, provocative and *terre à terre*. It is not the movements of the hips or the suppleness of the posteriors, nor the " provocative glances," which will prevail against the public's infatuation. " Taglioni, the queen of all, obliterates all your steps," exults the serious magazine. " Taglioni advanced and won the game with her first steps. Nothing more graceful or more captivating will ever be devised. . . . What a magnificent pride distinguished her poses, what a regal air dominated her gestures ! . . . She is still the Taglioni of the *Sylphide*, except that she is more daring, but this is ever tempered with a due sense of reserve and good taste. . . ."

A sketch by the Russian artist, Bassine, shows us the Gitana, invariably dressed in white and renouncing the tinsel of the Iberian dancer, to describe with rare breadth the grand curves of that spiral which is the actual formula for Spanish dancing, its abstract " concept." And the wooden *crotala* that her fingers once manipulated, to-day remain suppressed, " trinkets of sonorous inanity," in a case at the Musée de l'Opéra.

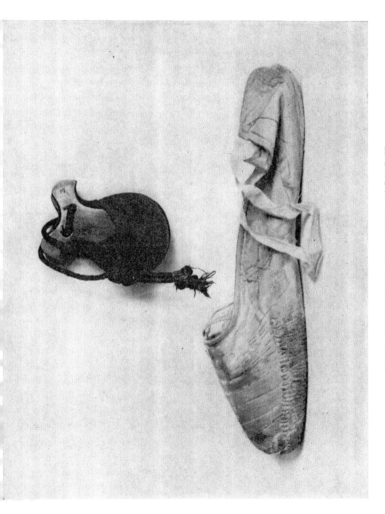

SOME SOUVENIRS OF MARIE TAGLIONI

A ballet shoe worn by the famous dancer, also the castanets used by her in "La Gitane"

(Musée de l'Opéra)

CHAPTER VI

" *Brillante, semi-aérienne,*
Obeissante à l'archet magique. . . ."
PUSHKIN.

Travels in Russia—The Cossacks and the *Kliukva*—First appearances
at St. Petersburg—The Imperial box—The Sylphide's popularity
displayed in print, vaudeville and Press—Farewells.

IN 1837, Marie Taglioni, who is now at the height of
her fame, leaves Paris with her father for St. Petersburg. Vainly does the young Queen Victoria attempt to
contend with Russia for the possession of her favourite
dancer and teacher. The prestige of the rouble, nay,
even the paper rouble, asserts its power. The Taglionis
make a contract for five years in consideration of
32,440 r. per season of six months ; three benefit performances for Marie, and two others for Philippe, complete
these imposing salaries ; for the receipts from these special
performances generally amounted to 25,000 r. Such
arguments must have prevailed with her, despite the
lamentations in prose and verse of her Parisian friends,
and the indignation of the " infernal box." The Sylphide
is leaving us ! Under this heading, the journal *Psyche*
gives vent to the general feeling : " And France, France
whom she leaves in mourning ? " The *Débats* is no less
emphatic : " Once more, farewell dancing shade "—sighs
Jules Janin in rhymed prose, or rather in abortive verse—

71

" who was our innocent joy, our chaste passion, our pleasure without remorse ! " The regular members of the Opéra audiences shared in this exaltation. An avalanche of bouquets covered the stage on the night of the farewell performance. " Do not ask what has been done to the Spring, it has been laid at the feet of Mlle. Taglioni." At this joyous period a critic still knew how to fashion a madrigal.

On the banks of the Neva, she was already impatiently awaited. " Tell the French," wrote Prince Odoevsky—a Hoffmanesque poet—to a friend, " that we have almost had to wait for her." The literary reviews worked up public opinion in Taglioni's favour. From her very arrival, busybodies kept the Paris public informed of her triumphs. Russia was then, as she actually has again become, a half-legendary country exciting the imagination. An example of the lightness with which certain travellers treat the things appertaining to that hyperborean empire has remained classic. Alexandre Dumas, in his *Impressions de Voyage*, describes Cossacks having tea " in the shade of a tufted *kliukva*." Now the *kliukva* is a modest little berry whose stalk measures a matter of centimetres.

Beneath its shade, too, will be hatched fantastic stories, such as how Taglioni made her entrance into the city of the Tsars escorted by a number of horsemen come to greet her ; Charles Maurice declares that the *mujiks*, on returning to their village, told how at the theatre they had seen a pale fairy enter the Imperial box ; also that the people lined with silver trees the route where her sleigh passed. But all these absurdly untrue stories reflect but one truth, the dancer's immense popularity.

Everything everywhere promised success. There were elective affinities between Taglioni's style and the spirit of the Russian ballet. Fifteen years before, the poet Pushkin had sung : " The soulful flight of the Russian Terpsichore." He summarised in advance the quintessence of the Taglionian genius ; soaring of the body, elevation of sentiment. Alas, it was not given to him to see her. It is Istomina, the Russian dancer, whom, in one of his

winged stanzas, he reveals to us, " flying like down before
Æolus's breath."

This cult of a semi-aerial dance, expressive of things
of the soul, had been inaugurated at St. Petersburg by
Charles Didelot, that misunderstood forerunner whom
Gardel knew how to keep out of the Grand Opéra of
Paris, by filling him with mortifications. Didelot had to
foot the bill in order to produce his *Flore et Zéphyre* at the
Opéra. He reigned supreme over the Imperial *corps de
ballet*, just as a half-century later Marius Petipa did the
same ; he had the gift of adapting French tradition to
Slav sensitiveness. Did not Lucian of Samosata already
attribute to the mysterious hyperboreans the magic power
of elevation ? He styles them *aitrobates* : people who
walk in the air.

All this militated in favour of the new-comer, to say
nothing of the aura in which her Parisian fame bathed her.
Often we see the bewildered critic borrow wholeheartedly
from the columns of the *Débats*. Announced for September 3rd, Taglioni's first appearance was postponed to the
6th, which raised the excitement to fever heat. The whole
town was in a flutter ; the Bolshoy Theatre had to turn
people away. The Sylphide[1] was acclaimed in a manner
at once enthusiastic and solemn ; she was recalled three
times. Soon madness reigned. The etiquette of the
theatre was transformed. Ladies contributed their applause
—an unprecedented licence. Flowers were thrown on to
the stage from the boxes, a form of homage as unknown
in Russia before 1837, as it had been new to Paris ten
years earlier ; the innumerable recalls were censured by
a few ill-tempered persons, and an official journalist could
not recover from seeing " young men, who had not attained
officer's rank, dare to shout and stamp."

---

[1] Schneitzhoeffer's ballet was not unknown to the St. Petersburg
public. It had been produced by the French *maître de ballet*, Titus,
on May 28th, 1835, with scenery by Roller, the famous chief machinist ;
French dancers such as Mlle. Croisette, MM. Frédéric and Fleuri assured
the success of the interpretation of the principal characters ; among
the sylphides of the *corps de ballet* may be noted Andreyanova, who was
called to succeed Taglioni in Russia.

But nothing proves this infatuation better than the popular print and the vaudeville. A lithograph by Jukovsky depicts the crowd before the box-office. " To-day it is the Taglionoff, a famous play, we must see that," so runs the comment of the Russian Gavarni. One fights before the window ; the coachman with his copper plaque on his back pushes aside the " barin," wearing an enormous " stove-pipe " hat, while the official goes off with a sprightly air, ticket in hand, and thieves pick the pockets of fanatic devotees. It can be seen, declares the former director of the repertory of the Imperial Theatres, how the Russians strained their resources to the utmost to give themselves the pleasure of spending their money for Taglioni's benefit. The Opera Company was a dead failure. Taglioni alone filled the house.[1]

Karatygin, the prolific vaudeville-writer, an inferior Scribe, did not fail to take the proffered opportunity. *Une Avant-Scène au Bénéfice de Taglioni* drew all St. Petersburg. It was the only piece which, by repercussion, filled the Comedy Theatre, which on other days was completely empty.

The sung couplets belauded the dancer, " whose least moment reveals an admirable soul. . . . But the tongue is powerless to say what she expresses with her feet." The audiences were such that thirty-seven performances of this trifle given during a first season were afterwards followed by sixty more. The piece was given by order on a Saturday, a day on which Russian actors never played ; it was revived at the Gatchina Palace for a private performance, the Emperor Nicholas I himself directing its production, an indirect homage to the admired dancer.

Because Taglioni had completely captivated the colossal autocrat with marble features ; that gloomy and implacable man, who filled his circle with terror, was conquered by the dancer's " seraphic idealism " ; his strained and solemn dignity surrendered to a charm supreme in

---

[1] She happens to fall ill, the *Northern Bee* informs us, and the most cruel spleen falls on the capital for these two interminable weeks. And there is a corresponding delirium when she appears with one arm still bandaged with silk.

that quality. When she was dancing, the Emperor was absent only on rare occasions, and she danced two hundred times in five seasons. To smooth the difficulties experienced by the management, he granted 32,000 r. from his privy purse to meet the dancer's demands. He presented the Sylphide to the Empress. Although a slave to etiquette, he actually left his box, in which he had placed a statuette of Taglioni, to go, without ceremony, and sit in the first row of the stalls in order to see better. Everywhere monarchs treated the Sylphide on an equal footing, although her kingdom was not of this world. And the Tsar's example was such that even Father Jacinthe, who was a monk and one of the sagest of the orthodox theologians of the period, could not resist the temptation to be present in a shuttered box at the *ballet blanc* called *La Fille du Danube*.

The Russian Press, although slightly reserved, not to say hesitating, on the morrow of Taglioni's appearance, did not hold aloof from the movement. The proofs rediscovered in the magazines of the period by M. Pleshchayev, the kindly historian of the Russian Ballet, and by the late M. Soloviev, the bibliophile and biographer of the Sylphide, bear testimony to an infatuation that was ever increasing. We retain that symptom of success; we hesitate to quote the texts. Everywhere the Muse of the romantic ballet was condemned to let loose the same verbosity. The commonplace phrase and stereotyped picture abounds in these effusions. And it would have been a thankless task to translate the article in the *Northern Bee*, the Russian critic having sought inspiration for both form and matter in J. J.'s extravagant notices in the *Débats*. " Her glory has surpassed that of Rubini and of Karatygin," exclaims the *Gazette Artistique*, in 1838; *bel canto* and tragic declamation were dethroned. One journalist, representing the Russian golden mean and solid common sense, stormed against the transports of the public. " This manner of celebrating should be reserved for victories or other happy events." But when, on the occasion of her benefit on January 16th, 1839, Taglioni, dressed in a blue satin sarafan, danced a Russian dance, the enthusiasm rose to an unprecedented height.

There can be no doubt that the poets could not remain idle. A translation had been made of a slender volume published at Paris under the title : *Les Adieux de Mlle. Taglioni*, an anthology of lyrics drawn from the dancer's album. The Russians did not count themselves beaten. A versifier, who made use of a pseudonym, sang for over four pages in verses crammed with mythological allusions, but revealing a certain sense of observation. A good poet, Prince Viazemsky, adorned with a quatrain Wright's engraving, after the drawing by General Kiel, depicting Taglioni's foot *piquant sur la pointe* and surrounded by clouds. A title recapitulated in French the meaning of the epigram drawn up in Russian : " *Pourquoi chausser une aile ?* "

This print far from exhausts Russia's contribution to the Sylphide's iconography. So far as we know, there remains no example of the busts and statuettes of the dancer which were manufactured by the " physionotype " process and put on sale in the halls of the Diorama. On the other hand, Razumikhin's lithograph after the drawing by Zelensky is an invaluable document. Contemporaries were struck by the resemblance which, to-day, we find just a little cruel. Taglioni is represented full length in her part of *La Fille du Danube*. She is standing on a balustrade ; behind her is seen the representation of the river into which she is about to fling herself ; she wears a garland of water-lilies and a laced bodice of mediæval cut. Zelensky profits by a pause to record her fleeting likeness. The remarkable sketches by Bassine, which are in the possession of Mme. Trefilova, the illustrious star of the Russian Ballet, endeavour to represent Taglioni in full flight. In the Russian academician's album, she is seen sometimes bounding with *grands jetés*, sometimes posing *en arabesque sur la pointe*, lightly leaning on her kneeling partner. These drawings are free and rapid sketches ; they displace air. One of these shows us the *pas* from *La Gitane*, the ballet created on November 23rd, 1838,

76

MARIE TAGLIONI IN "LA FILLE DU DANUBE"
From the drawing made at St. Petersburg by Bassine

which is a counterpart of the *Gypsy*; this *pas*, as we know, was to be the answer to Fanny Elssler's *Cachucha*. A very interesting lithograph by Timm, which, in the style of Célestin Nanteuil, shows us nine different scenes on the same stone, instructs us in regard to a ballet not yet given in France—*L'Ombre* (music by Maurer, first performed on November 28th, 1839). In the centre panel is depicted the scene of the mirror whose reflection is danced by understudies; the other miniatures depict Taglioni changed into a statue or throwing herself into a water-fall.

Five successive seasons will not detract one iota from her supremacy in the Northern Palmyra. If certain evil tongues begin to insinuate that she was no longer the same, other connoisseurs declare to their readers that, although everything fades and ages, even talent, Taglioni is an exception to the laws of nature. Who is right?

And, in this matter, can the impartiality of the better judge be trusted? From 1838, Théophile Gautier declares that Mlle. Taglioni, exhausted by endless travel, is no longer what she was; she has lost much of her lightness and elevation. "The princes and kings of the north," slyly insinuates old Théo, "in their imprudent and pitiless admiration have over-applauded her . . . they have made so many showers of flowers and diamonds fall upon her that they have weighed down her tireless feet. . . ." And he emphasises this theme and compares Marie of the graces to a bird with wet wings. Why does the critic set upon the Sylphide? We already know the reason for it. He sacrifices her to Fanny Elssler. Six years later, at the time of Taglioni's farewell to the Parisian public, he will completely change his mind. Then, he will find that not a single feather has dropped from her wing, and will punctuate with exclamation marks the description of her dance.[1] Undoubtedly, Gautier was the most honest man in the world; but his changes of opinion in regard to Taglioni are the outcome of the sentimental weaknesses of a great and fickle heart.

[1] It is true that, in going, Taglioni left the field open to Carlotta Grisi, Gautier's Péri.

Taglioni did not stray from St. Petersburg during her residence in Russia. Moscow beckoned to her. But the dancer having demanded 3,000 r. for each performance, with a benefit in addition, would not give way on this point. The journey was never made. Her engagement came to its conclusion. The ballet *Yetta, Reine des Elfrides* was produced for her farewell benefit on January 26th, 1842. During the last week she revived one of her parts each evening; this recapitulation, the chain of her successes, was the cause of the most tumultuous regrets. On March 18th, Taglioni definitely took leave of her Russian public. She was recalled eighteen times. Dissolving into tears, she addressed the audience in French : " For ever you will be engraved on my heart," said she, and promised to return. The emotion was so great that she had to repeat her farewell. Besides, the opera-houses closed during Lent ; hence, contrary to custom, another two Taglioni performances were given for the " unorthodox " public. Recalled thirty times, Taglioni repeated her speech in German. We know that she spoke several languages. The ladies of the *corps de ballet* decorated her dressing-room with flowers so that it resembled a conservatory.

Despite her promise, she was destined never to return. Her departure left an inexpressible void. Despite the flowering of Russian talents such as the Smirnovas and the Schlefogts, the ballet was completely forlorn. It took three years for people even to begin to forget her. The sale of her furniture afforded an epilogue to her triumphs. Everything that could serve as a memento of the Sylphide was seized upon. And with tears in their eyes the faithful begged, regardless of price, for a pair of those shoes which she had worn to conceal her wings.

CHAPTER VII

THE LIFE OF A WANDERING STAR

" Will the young folks ever see anything so charming, anything so classic, anything like Taglioni ? "—THACKERAY.

Taglioni at London—A chapter of the *Roman Comique*—Tribulations of a theatre manager—The celebrated *Pas de Quatre*—A question of precedence—Taglioni and the King of Prussia—A serenade—Decline and Retirement—The Sylphide's marriage—Clouded years —Taglioni's pupils—The singed butterfly—The death of Taglioni.

PARIS witnessed Taglioni's fame at its highest point ; her charm, however, radiated over the whole of Europe. We have recounted the dancer's first performances in her travels to Vienna and Stuttgart ; we have followed the sublime nomad to the Northern Palmyra, as St. Petersburg used to be styled poetically. But, missionary of the " Christian " dance *in partibus infidelium,* it was to England that she preached the gospel with the most constant zeal. And it is *in hoc signo* that the romantic ballet prevailed in London. From 1831 to 1847, each reappearance of Taglioni aroused enthusiasm. After her departure, this great saltatory fever died. The lyric art vanquished it ; the unpredecented infatuation for Jenny Lind, the Swedish Malibran, precipitated the decadence of the ballet whose existence in England was destined to remain precarious and its success intermittent. It had no roots in British soil, but had been grafted on the English stage by artists such as Albert and Noblet whom the

Restoration had loaned to " perfidious Albion." Taglioni made her first appearance, supported by Perrot, in *Flore et Zéphyre* and *La Bayadère.* Sheaves of prints strew her path, eloquent testimony to an unparalleled reputation.

But no other indication of true popularity is more significant than the bitterness of caricaturists. We have been able to find a pictorial pamphlet which attacks the Sylphide, without, however, naming her. It consists of an album of eight lithographs by Théophile Wagstaff, published at London, in 1836, under this title :

" *Flore et Zéphyr (sic), Ballet Mythologique dedié à . . .*"

Follows a vignette in which is seen Taglioni, treated with a cruelty reminiscent of Daumier, simpering with arms crossed upon her breast, and mouth split from ear to ear with a never-ending smile. But this series of caricatures, which throws into relief the contradiction between the sentiments which the characters are supposed to feel and the choregraphic expression they accord them, teaches us more about Didelot's style of composition and the dancer's technique than any number of flowery madrigals. Thus, Flore-Taglioni " deplores Zéphyre's absence " in an *adage* ; she is represented with her back to the crowded audience, at the moment of executing a *développé à la grande seconde*, the leg stretched to the height of the hip ; the scene of reconciliation reveals her to us in a most effective group, posing *en arabesque* on the knee of her partner, who has the other on the ground ; through the unkind deformation one can perceive the fine composition of the finale.

As at Paris, *La Sylphide* arouses the utmost enthusiasm ; a tour to the large provincial towns, such as Manchester or Liverpool, leads her to Perth, the mediæval city in the Highlands. Is it not the Scotland of faery which evoked Phillippe Taglioni's famous ballet ? Thus the faded country gentry crowd into the stalls. Everything is lacking : skilled orchestra, properties, *corps de ballet*, supers ; but enthusiasm supplies everything. One evening when *Nathalie, ou La Laitière Suisse* is billed, it is found that the dummy, upon which the whole plot centres, has been mislaid. " Pierre, you will be the dummy." And the faithful servant, duly shaved (his beautiful side-whiskers shed), saves the situation in the nick of time.

At London, the craze for Taglioni, an unhoped-for mascot, fails to extract from difficulties the impresario Laporte, struggling to establish a permanent opera on the banks of the Thames. He gives way after fifteen years' resistance and dies on the Continent from heart disease. He had agreed to pay Taglioni one hundred pounds for each performance. One evening, the unfortunate manager had been unable to collect even a penny. He countermanded the ballet. But this did not please the rowdy frequenters of the King's Theatre. "We want Laporte!" shouted the ringleaders. The manager came on the stage. "We want Taglioni!" they bellowed their loudest. "I cannot force her to come," retorted the poor man. "Pay her!" thundered the pit, advised of the occult reason for the change of programme. Later, Laporte having thrown in his hand, we owe to his successor, Benjamin Lumley, who for twenty years kept up the theatre, become "Her Majesty's" in honour of Queen Victoria, some reminiscences full of good humour and useful information.

Nothing in the years which followed detracted from the recognised supremacy of Taglioni, neither Fanny Elssler's abortive attack, nor the "Cerritomania" with which the second Fanny inflamed the dandies of "Fop's alley" (fashion required *balletomanes* to leave their stalls and fill the gangways), nor the welcome accorded to the Dane, Lucile Grahn, who, like Adèle Dumilâtre, belonged to the same "ideal school" as Taglioni's.

However, jealous of her fame, Taglioni dreams of retiring. Lumley has much ado to induce her to return to London in 1845, after two seasons of doubt. The skilful manager planned a great coup. He had decided to bring together in a *pas de quatre* the great dancers attached to his theatre—a formidable enterprise! Three years earlier, in order to arrange for Elssler and Cerrito to appear in a *pas de deux*, had it not been necessary to invoke the peremptory commands of the young queen? Everything

F

was in readiness to carry out the project which was to bring together Taglioni, La Cerrito, Lucile Grahn and Carlotta Grisi. Perrot was engaged to compose the dance; Carlotta was kept at Paris by rehearsals. To avoid delay, Lumley arranged for relays of horses between Paris and Calais, and chartered a steamboat with a special train in waiting at Dover.

Above all, it was a question of not offending any susceptibility. Each movement of each finger had to be calculated to a nicety, so as not to give the advantage to anyone. Each star had to shine in her own style without, however, eclipsing the others. Everything went splendidly; the rehearsals were almost ended, the bills were posted, when one day Perrot, in desperation, burst into the manager's room: "It is all over! There will be no *pas de quatre*!" It was found that when all was ready it was impossible to settle the order of the *soli*. The place of honour, the *last*, as in royal processions, had been unanimously conceded to Taglioni. But Carlotta refused to appear before Cerrito, and the latter before Grahn; there was no way of making them forgo their claims.

Lumley immediately devised a solution worthy of Solomon. The question of talent would be decided by the public. As to the order of the *soli*, he gave the preference to the *eldest*. The plan succeeded. On June 26th, 1845, the great event of the season took place.

The *Pas de Quatre* opened with an *adage* which grouped the famous rivals in a series of pictures. Taglioni made her entrance surrounded, almost carried, by her companions. One of Chalon's lithographs records another group; the dancers, one knee resting on the ground and holding hands, form a living hedge about Taglioni who, her arms *en couronne*, patters *sur place* on the tips of her toes. As to the *soli*, I believe I have been able to extract from the circumstantial account in the *Illustrated London News*, that Taglioni and Grahn executed *variations* of distance and elevation, one with that appearance of extreme simplicity which we know of, the other with a dashing impetuosity. Grisi appears to have performed a dainty

MARIE TAGLIONI IN "LE PAS DE QUATRE"
From the lithograph by A. E. Chalon

pizzicato, while the *jetés en tournant* of Cerrito, plump yet light, swept over the "boards." Nothing revealed to the public the internal discord which divided the participants in this competition.

At the end of each *variation* a rain of bouquets fell upon the stage ; the three others prettily helped the queen of the moment to reap that harvest of perfumed glory. And Cerrito had the pleasing thought to crown Taglioni with one of the garlands fallen at her feet. The following year again saw Taglioni, who had hesitated, procrastinated and at last consented to give one more farewell performance on the "boards" of Her Majesty's. For the first time she encountered a measure of opposition. Her detractors asserted that she was only the husk of what she had once been. Others declared that time had not touched her. The truth must lie between these two statements. Whatever it was, she remained the "big attraction" and, in the language of the box office, "brought the money in." Her admirers subscribed to offer her a souvenir worthy of her. They presented her with a group in chased silver representing herself and her partner in the ballet *Endymion*, created by her the previous year. This gift was valued at three hundred guineas.

However, the director was in search of ideas able to contend with the celebrated *Pas de Quatre*. Indeed, the *Pas des Déeses*, arranged on the theme of the Judgment of Paris, made a sensation. It brought together the same cast, with the exception of Carlotta. Saint-Léon danced the Trojan shepherd ; Perrot waved Mercury's *caduceus*. The plot was a simple one ; sometimes the goddesses fled from their mortal pursuer, sometimes they pursued him to secure the prophetic apple. Cerrito was acclaimed as, running towards the footlights, she turned in full flight in a *jeté battu* to seize the apple ; Grahn's *valse renversée* introduced the supreme finale of Taglioni, *sauté sur la diagonale*. The "three goddesses" were the talk of the hour, the "European event." Taglioni was the one topic of conversation at the club, dinner or ball. *Punch* based its jokes on the craze of the day.

In 1847, Taglioni, *the* Taglioni, records Lumley in his
memoirs, appeared once more in a revival of the famous
Pas de Quatre (Rosati taking Grahn's place) and achieved
one more triumph.[1]   There ensued the old demonstra-
tions, proofs of the former fever of enthusiasm, the old
cries, the old recalls.   But already the rising generation
was knocking at the door.   Lumley engaged a new Marie
Taglioni, the Sylphide's niece and Paul's daughter.

Marie, second of the name, was not twenty.

* * *

Many stories attest the renown enjoyed by the " priestess
of the chaste art " in the capitals of Germany.   *Les Adieux
de Mlle. Taglioni,* a slender volume of propaganda which
appeared in 1837, when Marie was about to leave for
Russia, the details for which had been supplied by the
dancer herself, did not exhaust the homage paid to the
Sylphide by the King of Prussia.   The ballet *Les Bayadères*
had drawn down upon itself a royal reproof as being an
offence against decency and good taste.   Taglioni invested
it with a modesty which disarmed the austere sovereign.
He came to a rehearsal and brought his family, which
had never been seen before.   " If I had been able, I should
have seen you in Paris," said the victor of 1814 to Taglioni.
" Sire, times have changed ; not everyone who wishes to
go to Paris can do so."   That should have been the reply.
Criticism followed in the footsteps of the soldier-king.
But even the liberals found " that Mlle. Taglioni's feet
enshrined a pious and profound thought " (Theodor
Mundt, quoted by M. Auguste Ehrhard).   Alone in her
opinion, Rahel Warnhagen, the celebrated woman who
ruled over a literary *salon* on the banks of the Spree, opens
a campaign against the intruder, to whom she refuses every
gift, in the name of her favourite dancer : Fanny Elssler.
. . . When, seventeen years after her first appearance at
the Kaerthner Thor, Taglioni returns to Vienna, she is

[1] Taglioni's son-in-law, a certain Prince Trubetskoy, had persuaded
the dancer to renounce the stage for good after a career of twenty-five
years.

received with enthusiasm. The first night she is recalled forty-two times. The crowd follows her to her abode. She is obliged to come out on the balcony. She throws flowers to her Viennese friends who struggle to secure these perishable mementoes.

Taglioni had already toured Italy in her first youth. But it is not until May 29th, 1841, that she treads, for the first time, the sacred boards of La Scala. In this connection we find in contemporary journals a flood of commonplace remarks and verse quotations. "Marie Taglioni has a form such as the artists of ancient Greece attributed to the Muses," and so on. But, setting aside this rubbish, the Sylphide enchanted the Milanese. On June 8th, the eve of her departure for Stockholm, where she was born, the whole orchestra came to offer her a serenade at the Albergo Marino, where she was staying. The sculptor Luigi Cossa was commissioned to design a medal of which one hundred copies were struck off and quickly bought up at the price of twenty francs each. Two years later Taglioni found less enthusiasm at Milan than before. In *Louise Strozzi*, the new ballet by Hus, the principal success went, so M. Gino Monaldi tells us, to the young mime Catte. Such are the main stages of that prodigious existence. Taglioni travels all over the world ; everywhere, she is received on bended knee. But all these attributes of glory and riches vanish like smoke. Physical decline, family troubles, ruin, everything goes against her, a heavy price to pay for fame. London, in 1847, bestowed on her her last laurel. The dancer had the courage to abdicate. The woman still had thirty-seven years to live.

"Do not speak to me any more of your old Taglioni, that sylphide of forty-six who is always pitched at the heads of other dancers," exclaims one of the characters in the *Petits Mystères de l'Opéra*, published in 1844. When she was twenty-three, officious people made the young vestal eighteen. Albéric Second spitefully adds six years to the woman of forty. For Charles de Boigne, she was, at that time, no more than a shadow of her former self. "The Sylphide is quite forgotten nowadays," he declares in his *Petits Mémoires de l'Opéra*, published in 1856, and he begins to hum the chorus of Béranger's "*grand'mère.*"

The public, like a big ungrateful child, was not the only one to forget her. . . .

"Here is the queen, the goddess of these spheres, Taglioni the ethereal," exclaims the same writer in a tone of banter. "But what do I see? Has she not a chain riveted to her wing? Alas! the Sylphide was married in the second *arrondissement* before the mayor." Taglioni had married, in 1832, Count Gilbert de Voisins, one of Dr. Véron's familiars. "The too notorious husband of the celebrated Taglioni" has been severely criticised by his contemporaries. De Boigne is of the opinion that the legitimate spouse of the Sylphide has been over maligned; he was a true nobleman, although a fine melter of money; this unhappy union lasted but three years.

In 1852, a thoughtless invitation of the Duc de Morny brought the separated couple together at a dinner party. "Tell me, who is that blue-stocking who speaks all languages?" asked the impertinent nobleman of his neighbour. Outrage or forgetfulness, this oft-related story has the appearance of truth, and depicts all the bitterness of a disappointed grandee. M. de Voisins, Vice-Consul of France at Figueroa, in Spain, died in 1863.

To the premature effects of age were added the humiliations of poverty. In a career of twenty-five years, Taglioni had earned and squandered millions. In a work, published in 1855, containing a list of former members of the Académie de Danse who had become titled and wealthy, Castil-Blaze still includes Taglioni, lady of a manor near Lake Como, owner of a palace at Venice. This prosperity was not lasting. Did she speculate, was she extravagant, ill-advised, or unlucky? No one can tell.

We only know that, after her retirement, she had to earn her own living laboriously and pitifully. At London she led a life of privation. "It was a sad sight to see her, white-haired," writes a contemporary, "conducting an English school, in the winter at Hyde Park, in the summer at Brighton, and accompanied by an old Italian violinist, teaching society dances and deportment to the stuck-up daughters of the gentry."

A link still existed between Taglioni and the house in the Rue Le Peletier where she had reigned; her pupils on whom she lavished her best, more than once enabled a conception of her own to triumph at the Opéra.[1] Her personal affection was bestowed on that poor Emma Livry, who died at the age of twenty-one following on terrible burns, the muslin in her costume catching fire at a rehearsal. There arose a rumour that Taglioni would reappear on the stage, after fourteen years' retirement, on the occasion of Livry's first appearance in 1858. There was no truth in it, but it was for that beloved child that Taglioni composed, with the aid of the skilled librettist Saint-Georges, a *ballet-pantomime* in two acts, *Le Papillon*, for which Offenbach wrote the music. The action passed in a Caucasus of fantasy, where *ballet blanc* alternated with oriental dances. In it, Livry shone notably in a *Lesghinka*, a Circassian *pas* danced with Mérante and which, though thirty years after, was her *Tyrolienne*. She took the part of Farfalla, whom " the wicked fairy Hamza changes into a butterfly," and it was not a commonplace choregraphic compliment, according to Théophile Gautier. She had inherited imponderable lightness and silent flight from her preceptor. Thin, almost emaciated, with a bony profile, Livry embodied in the extreme the physical type of the dancer of elevation as revealed by Taglioni. She suffered no more painful loss than the death of her double, in whom she hoped to live again.

This affection she passed on later to Mlle. Salvioni, whose defence she undertook on the occasion of a revival of *Le Dieu et la Bayadère*, in a letter of expostulation dated January 14th, 1856, and addressed to the editor of a paper I have not been able to trace. " I myself trained that young artist," she declares with considerable dignity. " I

[1] We find, moreover, at the Opéra, in the decade following her retirement, an heiress to her name, the *première danseuse* Taglioni, whose real name was L. Fuchs, who distingished herself in the *soli* in *Le Juif Errant*. Was she a relative, godchild or pupil of her whose name she borrowed? I cannot say.

have taught her the traditions of a part which will remain one of my most cherished memories." And she soundly rates the journalist whom she accuses of lacking in goodwill and of being very thoughtless; the culprit had let it be known that Salvioni had aroused little interest at the rehearsals. During the same year Salvioni created *La Source*, Delibes' first ballet.

The reader is already aware that the choregraphic dynasty of the Taglionis did not end with Marie's retirement. Her brother, Paul, born at Vienna in 1808, trained like her at Paris, and married at an early age to a young German dancer, was successively attached as *maître de ballet* to theatres in London and Naples; at Berlin he held the post of director of ballet for twenty years. He arranged a great number of ballets which had a vogue: *Ondine*, *Théa*, *Satanella*, *Plick et Plock*. His daughter, Marie, whose delicate beauty and whose many proofs of hereditary talent are attested by contemporary prints, made her first appearance at London in 1847. "*Prima ballerina*" of the Royal Opera, Berlin, she retired in 1866, the year in which she married Prince Josef von Windisch-Graetz; she died on April 27th, 1891. With her passing, the admirable choregraphic line came to an end.

Marie Taglioni, the elder and real one, died at Marseille on April 27th, 1884, at the age of eighty. In her passage to the tomb she preceded by seven months her sole rival, Fanny Elssler. We should completely ignore her last days if the dancer's grandson, the novelist Gilbert de Voisins, had not preserved in pages of an exquisite delicacy the "wonderful memory" he retains of "Grandmamma." This memento is not free from little errors of fact; but the octogenarian's silhouette appears singularly lifelike and intimate: "A very old lady who was never pretty, but whose expression remained captivating. . . . I see her again, attired in a black silk dress with flounces, her bodice fastened at the throat with a cameo-brooch. I see again those little ear-rings, her luxuriant white hair, plaited over her temples." So writes he who was the last to kiss the beloved, wrinkled features of her who had once been the

MARIE TAGLIONI IN " LE PAS DES DEESSES "
From the lithograph by A. E. Chalon
Saint-Léon
Cerrito   Taglioni   Rosati

Sylphide. At that time he was only a child. But that smiling expression in repose which He found on the lips of the dead woman likewise penetrates the pages—affectionate to the point of devotion—which the grown-up man has dedicated to the dancer, Marie Taglioni.

CHAPTER VIII

SYLPHIDIANA

" Ronds de jambes et ports de bras sur lesquels on pourrait faire de longs poèmes."—THÉOPHILE GAUTIER.

Legend and truth—Taglioni's poetic crown—A Press campaign—Stories about the Sylphide—Diplomatic illnesses—Quarrels with the *claque* —Was Marie a good comrade ?—Contradictory statements—Her correspondence : its style, spelling and wit—The summing-up of our investigations.

ONE cannot but be astonished at the writers who, in investigating birth certificates, documents and correspondence, have the singular presumption to pride themselves on reconstructing the personality of an artist, or of a " lady of yester-year." Everything emanating from such sources of investigation merely gives what the person in question wished herself to relate to a third party. If this be so, how can one distinguish between what *appears to be* and what *is*? Have we a clear vision of the characters and manners of the private lives of our most famous contemporaries ? Should we fulfil in regard to ourselves the philosopher's dictum : " Know thyself " ? Certainly not. And yet we judge the departed, whom we have never met, with the peremptory assurance of Minos and his two infernal colleagues !

In regard to Marie Taglioni, the object of our retrospective solicitude, we should like to employ a method more circumspect and also more respectful. We shall group, without wishing to come to a conclusion, the scattered and often contradictory information regarding her public and private career which we possess, and collate the evidence which is sometimes at variance, leaving it entirely to the reader's intelligence to decide in the last instance the authenticity and human value of these gleanings.

At first, we see the Sylphide's silhouette become transparent through the incense of poetic homage, then change comically or spitefully through the deforming glass of caricature. Whether she be praised or slandered, we shall always find some trace of her.

According to the prevailing fashion, Marie Taglioni possessed an album in which eminent guests at her *salon* paid their tributes in madrigals and well turned, although sometimes halting, quatrains. Musicians and *virtuosi,* Spontini and Meyerbeer, Thalberg and Donizetti, inscribe their precious signatures with some bars of music. I do not know what has become of that golden book, but a slender volume published in 1837 culls some petals from that poetic crown.

Méry, the petulant fantastic from Marseille, who, in the *Monde Dramatique*, extols Taglioni in octosyllabic verses, rises to the solemnity of the Alexandrine in order to praise her the more :

> *Elle était cette fois la sylphide rêvée,*
> *Que, sous le ciel d'Ecosse, un poète a trouvée,*
> *Divinité qui suit les pâtres au sillon,*
> *Aime les laboureurs, visite les chaumières,*
> *Et pendant la veillée, agite les lumières*
> *Avec son vol de papillon.*
>
> *Regardez-la courir ! Rien de mortel en elle.*
> *On craint de la blesser lorsqu'on touche son aile :*
> *Quand elle prend son vol, les regards soucieux*
> *Semblent la retenir au sol qu'elle abandonne. . . .*

It is the Sylphide again,

> *Du manoir écossais c'est le lutin femelle*

who inspires Mlle. Elise Talbot to make numerous easy

rhymes. Jules Canonge, a bard from Provence, addresses pompous stanzas to her " chaste majesty." A certain Léon Lenoir intones in her honour a semi-religious poem which seems to parody the angelic greeting :

> *Ah ! sois notre salut, vierge blanche, pieuse,*
> *Colonne de cristal, étoile radieuse . . .*

E. Demart fashions on *La Fille du Danube* a ballad in Victor Hugo's manner, which Adolphe Adam sets to music and of which 5,000 copies are sold. England, in turn, makes her contribution to the anthology by means of the stanzas written by the poet F. Bayley to accompany Chalon's prints. The exhibition of Barre's statuette of Taglioni inspires versifiers anew, and Méry seizes on the occasion to sing again of the

> *Nymphe du céleste jardin.*

It is fitting to detach from this lyric offering, in which mediocrity and pomposity abound, the impromptu that, taking for text the *Pas de l'Ombre* which Taglioni danced at the Opéra on the occasion of her farewell performances, Alfred de Musset writes in her album (1844) :

> *Si vous ne voulez plus danser,*
> *Si vous ne faites que passer*
> *Sur ce grand théâtre sombre,*
> *Ne courez pas après votre ombre*
> *Et tâchez de nous la laisser . . .*

And Théodore de Banville, while deploring, in his *Odes Funambulesques* (1857), the decline of the Opéra, will recall with melancholy that :

> *Ici Taglioni, la fille des Sylphides,*
> *A fait trembler son aile au bord des eaux perfides. . . .*

Composers were equally polite towards the famous dancer ; they wrote quadrilles and gavottes in her honour and went so far as to attribute the composition to her. Giacomo Meyerbeer composed the music for *La Fille de l'Air*, a poem dedicated to the abbess of *Robert le Diable*. Johann Strauss the younger, the famous Viennese conductor, made sure of the success of one of his valses by dedicating it to Taglioni, the cover being decorated with a pretty, engraved portrait of the dancer.

* * *

The more Taglioni inspired the dreams of poets, the more her indescribable ascendancy over the public galled the envious and made evil tongues chatter. A number of stories were spread which sought to show the immeasurable vanity of the dancer, jealous of her precedence, and also the caprices, often disastrous, by which she drove her managers to distraction. These *ana* reveal her avid for gain, avaricious, and inordinately jealous of the success of others. In examining these charges a considerable amount must be deducted for rancour and the interested intrigues of rivals.

To test this, one has only to follow, in the columns of the *Courrier des Théâtres*, the turns of fortune in the daily war of attrition which Charles Maurice, her former ally and censer-bearer, waged for six months at the rate of three or four ironic echoes, insulting or defamatory, daily. The length of Marie's arms alone gave rise to a hundred unkind jests. "While dancing yesterday before the public," records the dry joker, "La Taglioni put her garter on again without bending down." Sometimes he makes puns on the "*bras de mer*," sometimes he announces that, in a piece in course of rehearsal, Taglioni is going to dance a *pas de châle* "with her arms" as the only property. This piece, the failure of which he tried to ensure by all manner of means, is none other than *La Sylphide ;* after the event, he will be found fretfully to acknowledge its success. While trying to humiliate the dancer by vulgar plays on words, he made a special set at her father, Philippe, "decomposer" of ballets, to whom he attributes every platitude and pilferage.

"The Taglionis are bug-bears at the Opéra ; however well they are weeded, they always spring up again. . . .

One day weariness gave birth to M. Taglioni." Such were the amenities which the journalist revived every morning. Philippe Taglioni, moreover, is the critic's pet aversion. The teacher and factotum of his daughter, a clever strategist, he was, if we may credit de Boigne who knew him, " subtle, adroit, well-mannered, resolute, a fanatical father and choregrapher," blindly obeyed by Marie, and knowing how to beard the most stubborn managers. Good old Duponchel, Véron's successor, who had been among his partisans in former days, had to put up with Marie Taglioni's whims. He had announced for the second time the dancer's reappearance, already once postponed, when a message from Taglioni warned him on the very day, about noon, that she was ill, and that it would be impossible for her to dance that evening. In desperation, the manager ran to the little flat in the Rue Grange-Batelière. The father of the young invalid received him with tears in his eyes : " What can you expect ? " he bewailed, " her chilblain has reopened." By degrees, the bulletins regarding her health indicated a slight improvement. " The wound has healed," declared Philippe, to every inquirer. But, towards the month of July, the trouble grew worse ; the regular dancer of the Opéra was expected at the " Queen's " in London, where she was paid for each performance.

It is very possible that this story, too good for the gossip-writer not to take advantage of it, had been inspired by the campaign of innuendo opened by Maurice : " M. Taglioni," chaffed the journalist, " has broken an engagement with his daughter's indisposition. It was agreed in this treaty that recovery would take place in such a way that *La Sylphide* would not have been given more than four or five times before it was time for the dancer to take her holiday. There is even a penalty equivalent to the large amount which they hope to get to buy back the holiday." And he gleefully discourses on the corns, bunions and chilblains of the *"malade imaginaire."* Even when these indispositions were not the result of diplomacy, she remained a living and indecipherable

AN AUTOGRAPH LETTER OF MARIE TAGLIONI
(*From the collection of C. W. Beaumont*)

problem for the doctors. Her famous knee trouble, without either redness or swelling, which kept her more than nine months on her couch, has remained historic. Time being a fine doctor, the knee became well of itself and very naturally after the birth of a pretty pink and white baby. That elegant euphemism, " knee trouble," remains a classic phrase in the parlance of the green room. Nevertheless, in 1837, Duponchel, fearing another relapse, never renewed the contract, and so Taglioni only reappeared at the Opéra for certain performances.

Other stories were spread about Taglioni's connivance, or rather contentions, with the *claque*, which, under Véron's management, had become a constitutional power. Théophile Gautier devoted an article in the *Presse* to a droll eulogy of Auguste, the great chief of the *claque*, a collaborator very much in touch with managements and authors. Auguste deserves a book to himself! We find the echo of this scandal in a pamphlet, otherwise inane, which the author devotes to reproving the evil brood of *claquers*, his honest creators of successes, while blaming the artistes who solicit their services. These effusions, respects, excuses of the delirious author are addressed to Taglioni and to Noblet, whose names are interlaced on the title-page. When Charles Maurice goes to war against the " Taglioni coalition " and the trumpeters in the newspapers, he attributes the greater part of the dancer's success to the members of the *claque*. Some disabused contemporaries state that in fifteen years Mlle. Noblet expended over 50,000 francs on stimulating the enthusiasm of Auguste's legionaries. As to whether Taglioni benefited from that generally admitted expenditure, nothing is less doubtful. But her sovereignty over the public did not depend on these paid admirers. A hundred proofs which have come down to us indicate how spontaneously Taglioni, the sublime incarnation of the spirit of an age, had been adopted by all classes. Among a hundred other curiosities and references, I shall cull this little scene of provincial life, referring to her stay at Bordeaux, in October and November, 1828, in the dawn of her glory.

"The last time she appeared, she was thrown some garlands with the following quatrain addressed by Voltaire to Mlle. Sallé, whose talents and modesty were undoubtedly as discouraging as those of Mlle. Taglioni :

De tous les cœurs et du sien la maîtresse,
Elle alluma des feux qui lui sont inconnus,
De Diane elle est la prêtresse
Dansant sous le nom de Vénus.

"These verses were applauded with such enthusiasm that the author of the incident, fearing to be taken for a plagiarist, shouted from his box in a stentorian voice : ' Don't forget to say, idiot, that they are by Voltaire ! ' "

While everything confirms the unblemished authenticity of her glory, certain remarks, true or fabricated, seem to prove the Sylphide's intolerance for, or morbid jealousy of, the success of others. Perrot having obtained a great personal success in *La Revolte au Sérail*, Taglioni (recounts M. Auguste Ehrhard, according to the *Ménestrel*) made a frightful scene : " Is it not dreadful," she cried, " that a male dancer should obtain more applause than I ! What treachery, what infamy." Despite the objurgations of Véron, who sharply rebuked the careless M. Auguste, she continued to sob, crying : " What a fine reward for all my sacrifices ! " Fanny Elssler's biographer concludes without further consideration that Taglioni " carried to excess the worst faults of the barnstormer." Again, we must not forget to weigh the value of green-room gossip and to distinguish prudently between truth and legend, between actual fact and an amusing caricature. There are not lacking little incidents which show Taglioni as a good friend, generous to the point of prodigality, and helping someone much less important than herself to benefit from her own success. At St. Petersburg, a faithful witness tells us, her modesty and tenderness made her loved by everyone. To the dancers she had been a true sister. So tears flowed in streams on the departure of " dear Terpsichore." All this brings us to the formula propounded by Charles de Boigne : "The foot alone was exacting, jealous and difficult ; the heart was sound."

* * *

Do Taglioni's autograph letters afford any less fallacious elements of appreciation regarding her character ? Hardly. A certain disparity between tone and style may be observed. Taglioni's correspondence, scattered over the whole world, has never been collected. The known possessors of important files reserve publication, nay, even the communication of their contents.

A long letter addressed to M. Zagoskine, director of the Moscow Opera, seems to reveal a conspicuous sense of business and a scarcely poetic sharpness in the discussion, which amounts to vulgar bargaining. Taglioni asks 5,000 r. for each performance and defends this fee by rather commonplace arguments. "You will understand, General," she apologises, "how much it costs me to speak of my interests at such length, the world is made so, pleasure never goes alone (November 23rd, 1838) . . ." But, in analysing the style and strictly correct spelling of this official communication and comparing it with her private letters, one is forced to conclude that Taglioni at most held the pen while recopying the draft by Philippe, a skilful and tenacious impresario.[1]

Taglioni generally wrote in French, without, however, always avoiding the pitfalls of grammar, and disposing of punctuation marks in an arbitrary manner. If she knew more on this head than her rival, Fanny, she none the less spelt certain words in her own way, writing: "*tourmants*," "*excecive*," "*decorts*." At bottom, one cannot help discovering in certain of her letters to her Parisian friends, an irritating kind of pawkiness and a thinly disguised causticity with which she inveighs against an applauded

[1] Here is a letter in French from Fanny, collated exactly with the original: "*Bon jour, Gentz, tu es bien étonner, que je t'écriez en français, n'est-ce pas ? tu vois comme je suive tes conseilles. . . .*" (August, 1830). It is true that Gentz had just taught her the elements of the French language, but the spelling of her letters in German is almost as fantastic.

97

rival : " Laporte is anxious to engage him (Perrot) "—she writes in a letter from London, published by M. Henri Prunières in the *Revue Musicale*—" but for nothing, and he doesn't want to go for nothing like Guerra did, who gave his wife into the bargain and even that bargain was no great catch." Altogether, her letters deal mainly with her success, on the sums earned by her, and the mistakes or vexations of others upon which she complacently dilates. Thus, in an epistle dated August 20th, 1835, she delights in slandering, not without a little touch of pity, her personal enemy, Fanny, who, at London, has just created *L'Ile des Pirates*, arranged by Henri. " Altogether, there was not much interest in the proceedings," she resumes : " the Elsslers wore themselves out to little purpose." From the passages quoted, it seems that Taglioni was not magnanimous in her triumph. On the other hand, in her days of trial, she knew how to retain a resigned sweetness and a serenity of soul proof against everything, which are reflected in her replies to a little game of questions and answers which the septuagenarian gave with a good grace. We are indebted to Mme. Anna Pavlova for communicating to us this touching and harrowing document.

" What is your chief characteristic ? " asks the questionary, printed in English, of she who was the Sylphide.

" Resignation in adversity."

" Your idea of misery ? "

" Something sent by God to test us."

" Your favourite food and drink ? "

" Bread every day and a glass of water drawn from a clear spring."

" What is your present state of mind ? "

" Rather cheerful."

One hardly knows how to resist that last characteristic when one ponders on all that life had given and taken away from Marie Taglioni, the dethroned queen.

CHAPTER IX

THE ANATOMY OF THE SYLPHIDE

" Regardez-la courir.   Rien de mortel en elle."

MÉRY.

Was Taglioni beautiful ?—Contradictory evidence—The lithograph of
the Romantic Era—Sketch for a portrait—A sublime monster—
Taglioni's " trade "—Her style—Her influence—Decline of the male
dancer—Feminine romanticism.

" THE famous *ballerina* Taglioni came to St. Petersburg with her father, a little old man," relates a
former pupil of the Imperial Theatre School, in her
Memoirs. " She came to the school to do her exercises.
The director and his assistants paid the foreigner every
attention.   Taglioni was very plain and excessively thin;
her little sallow face was covered with tiny wrinkles.   I
blushed for the pupils who, after class, surrounded Taglioni
and said to her in compassionate tones :   ' What an ugly
mug you've got ; how wrinkled you are ! '   Taglioni,
who imagined she was listening to compliments, tossed
her head, smiling, and murmured in French : ' Thank you,
children.' "

Another of these frolicsome pupils sounds a different
note in her *Recollections* :   " We looked upon her," she
declares, " as a goddess.   She was not what one would
call a beauty, but she had supremely elegant manners.   She
was quite ethereal."

Despite their difference in tone, the two extracts quoted

99

both indicate a prematurely faded young woman (at the time of her visit to Russia, Taglioni was barely thirty-three), whose charm lay more in her manner than in her physical attractions. She had nothing of the statuesque beauty of Fanny Elssler. Of the attributes of a pretty woman, she had nothing beyond what was required to make a great dancer.

"That a dancer, thirty years ago, should have been able to bring about a revolution in the art of dancing which is still effective, is in itself astonishing," declares the author of *Petits Mémoires de l'Opéra*; " but that this dancer, this great revolutionary, should have been an ill-made woman, almost hump-backed, without beauty and without any of those striking exterior advantages that command success, amounts to a miracle." . . .

Another anecdote, related by M. Ehrhard, the excellent biographer of Taglioni's rival, Elssler, has it that when Taglioni's father took her to Coulon's class, her fellow-pupils made fun of her, saying : " How can that little hunchback ever learn to dance ? " This is another version of Hans Christian Andersen's story of the " Ugly Duckling," who, despised by her kind, one day turns out to be a swan, and spreads her white wings.

The celebrated ugliness of the actor Lekain played a considerable part in his posthumous fame. The memory of his ravaged mask survives where innumerable cameo-like profiles have been forgotten in the limbo of time. Were not the Sylphide's supposed infirmities the very marks of her genius ? What difference did it make if, when she flew to the ground, the spread of her wings, like those of the albatross in *Les Fleurs du Mal*, prevented her from walking ?

In this wasted body of paradoxical proportions everything functioned, everything was in accordance with some secret design, favourable to soaring flight. There are musical instruments, violins fashioned by an Amati or a Stradivarius, dwellings for souls, which have the contour and reactions of a living being. By a miracle of contrariness, the divine craftsman fashioned of Marie Taglioni, a

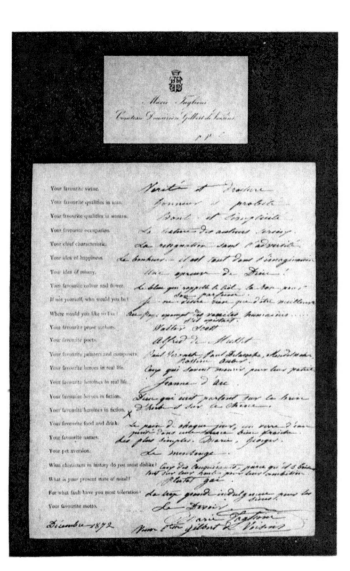

MARIE TAGLIONI'S AUTOGRAPH REPLIES
to a Questionary
(*From the collection of Mme. Anna Pavlova*)

woman without any sensual appeal, owing to her emaciated and bruised frame, an incomparable instrument, which, setting metaphors aside, we shall endeavour to take to pieces and describe.

But at this juncture our literary sources cease to be reliable. The opinions of her contemporaries are eloquent, but never concrete and explicit. " Light, ethereal, seraphic," are all very well ; but such epithets merely enumerate the attributes of an object ; they do not describe it. Circumlocutions abound. In praising Taglioni, poets and critics alike perceive nothing of the being of flesh-and-blood ; they conduct us through " a forest of symbols." Each gesture and each bound are recorded figuratively.

Is it surprising that a Jules Janin should fail to find the right word to give life to his portrait ? But even Gautier, the vigorous craftsman of *Fusains et Eaux-fortes*, did not succeed in condensing the vaporous vision. When he is dealing with Carlotta Grisi, " *la belle dame sans merci*," he gives an impression of her which, despite his emotion, has all the precision of an official document :

" Carlotta . . . is fair, or at least auburn. She has blue eyes, of an extraordinary limpidity and softness. Her mouth is small, dainty and childlike. . . ."

And so on. When he undertakes to depict Mlle. Fanny Elssler for the subscribers to the *Figaro*, we not only learn that the Florindo of the *Diable Boiteux* is tall, supple and well set-up, but also that she has " slender wrists and dainty ankles," that " her knee-caps are well defined, stand out in relief, and make the whole knee beyond reproach," and that " her hands are slim and delicate."

But, when he turns to Taglioni, our poet no longer says : " She is this or that," but : " She makes us think of . . ." And he proceeds to draw comparisons. Amid that cloud of white muslin, he no longer regards her as a beautiful and desirable feminine body, but as an allusion to something inexpressible in words. Faced with such a bankruptcy of description, we are obliged to have recourse to pictures.

There is an innumerable quantity of portraits of Taglioni,

both drawn and engraved. The iconography of her in Russian, prepared by N. V. Soloviev, gives seventy-one items ; and this list is far from complete. So we must again search through this bulging portfolio in order to obtain a reasonable likeness of the Sylphide.

The print of the romantic era is as conventional as the designs used by Ionian potters. Allowance must be made for the stylisation which reduced the lithographs of dancers to a type conforming to the fashion of the day and stamped with a commonplace banality.

There is nothing of value to be gleaned from the official portrait by Grevedon. It is a full-face portrait in which he strives to treat Taglioni in the manner of a vignette from a *Keepsake* ; this document is of interest merely on account of the pains taken to render the details of this wax doll's head-dress. The print by Jean Gigoux, the fertile illustrator of *Gil Blas*, is little better, being executed in the same conventional manner and " one of a series." There are some more authentic engravings that afford us a few details. But the truth is to be found in the work of one painter only, that of A. E. Chalon, of the Royal Academy, London (who also had the honour of being hung in the National Gallery). His *Six Sketches*, as well as his coloured lithograph, dated 1845, of the famous *Pas de Quatre*, which marked the fullest development of the romantic ballet just before it began to decline, do suggest the idea of Taglioni as we had imagined her. Chalon, a man of perception, did not attempt to correct the natural features of his model to make them conform to some abstract ideal. Hence we can always turn to him when in doubt. Thanks to such testimony, it is possible to reconstruct a hypothetical portrait of Taglioni.

The very first thing that strikes us about the Sylphide's physiognomy is the very high and slightly domed forehead, which, rather than the eyes, illumines the face and extends the irregular, oval form suggested by the wide jaws and short, sharp chin. The smooth bands of chestnut hair leave the temples free. The nose is thin and long ; the narrow lips are raised at the corners in a smile. The curve of the eyebrows is very flat; the eyelids, weary and pallid, droop over hazel eyes that are fairly small.

Her complexion has no bloom; the skin, which is exceedingly delicate, is jaded from the use of cosmetics. The expression of her face is serene, though tinged with melancholy, and she has the appearance of great intelligence. To be frank, Marie Taglioni looks like a sickly old maid who has suffered many woes and made up her mind to take the veil.

Her head is small, set upon a long, undulating neck, the swan neck beloved of poets, which painters such as a Domenico Veneziano or a Pisanello, in their portraits, bestowed on high-born Tuscan ladies of the fifteenth century. This sinuous neck joins the sloping shoulders in a lovely curve; the falling-away of the bust makes the back of the "little humpback" seem round-shouldered. The collarbones are prominent; the bosom is small and low; the waist short and delicate, a wasp waist. The slender, tapering arms are abnormally long and end in very small wrists and slim fingers. In a foot-note to his *Manual of Classical Theatrical Dancing*, the well-known teacher Enrico Cecchetti tells us that Taglioni's father taught her to cross her arms in order to conceal this defect; in this way an unsightly blemish yielded a charm the more. On the other hand, the choreographer Saint-Léon, who partnered Taglioni, declares that: "there were *balletomanes* who took exception to the way she generally held her arms in a low position, quite contrary to the custom of the other dancers; they also criticised her deportment, for she held her body much further forward that was customary in the dancing schools of that day."

At the same time, her legs are too long in proportion to the rest of her body. The "portrait" which we have of one of these legs shows it to be extremely well-shaped, with the exception of a slight thickening of the calf, the characteristic blemish found in the professional dancer, the result of muscular strain. The instep, delicately fashioned, smooth and slender, seems to move under the silken tights. The foot is long and pointed, the instep arched, the toe-joints elongated, the sole of the foot so curved that it seems to be breaking the ballet shoe. Achille Devéria's celebrated lithograph, after Barre's statuette, represents, with a happy stretch of imagination, the Sylphide dancing in bare feet over the flowers of her celestial garden. The big toe seems to be short, the other toes quite long. Is this conformation based on fact ? Or is it a concession to some " ideal of beauty " applied to the foot of a goddess ?

But the most important question of all concerns that indescribable foot which Victor Hugo likened to a wing. Was it small ? In his exquisite *Souvenir de Marie Taglioni, Danseuse*,[1] M. Gilbert de Voisins, her respectful grandson, recalls, among many memories, a scene where a young friend who was calling on the lady who had been the Sylphide, wondered at the " slender elegance, the incredible narrowness " of the shoes preserved by the dancer in a little amaranthine casket, and declared that it seemed impossible that they could ever have fitted any woman's foot.

Thanks to the munificence of Mme. Robert Brussel, the Musée de l'Opéra has a duplicate of this family treasure. An examination of this winged sandal does not entirely confirm the legend of Cinderella's slipper. In fact, the shoe of Fanny Elssler, Taglioni's rival, is not only smaller, but noticeably shorter. Taglioni's foot, besides being extremely narrow, is very long in proportion. If it be compared with one of the shoes that belonged to some famous beauty, such shoes as those preserved in the Musée de Cluny, it does not remind us of the pattens of a Chinese beauty, or of the silken mules of the Princesse de Lamballe, but rather of the black satin slippers once worn by the Empress Josephine.

It is certainly not the foot of a pretty woman, a coquettish *bibelot* of flesh and blood, mincing along with tiny steps ; it is not the kind of foot one would choose to cross a ball-room with, or trip to a lover's tryst.

The conclusions to be drawn from this comparative

---

[1] This essay is also included in the author's book: *Les Miens*, Paris, 1926—*Tr.*

study of the documentary evidence and exhibits are almost self-evident. In general, our inquiry narrows down to an individual singularly lacking in physical attractions, whose anatomy violates all our preconceived ideas of feminine beauty. With very little exaggeration, Taglioni could be called deformed !

This being so, how can this dancer's fascination be explained ? It is a fact that, although small of stature, she appeared tall to those critics who sought to express " the characteristic qualities of her beauty." Stage lighting, coupled with the glamour of the theatre, can of course do much ; but all this did not prevent the " spirit-like arms " of the emaciated Fitz-James from arousing laughter. The mystery remains, only to be explained by the fact that plastic perfection and choregraphic beauty are two separate things.

In a statue, we admire a body in stable equilibrium, resting on its base, invoking the immutable harmony of masses and planes. Dancing is a kinetic art which, instead of avoiding the movement that displaces the lines of the composition, traces figures in space only to erase them at once. In dancing of the classic school, these ideal figures attain a geometric purity of outline where there is a play of sweeping curves around intersections of straight lines. A vertical line intersected at a determined angle by two parallels—such, for instance, is the outline of an *arabesque sur la pointe*, in which exhibition of shifting equilibrium Taglioni excelled. The *pointe tendue* extends the vertical line of equilibrium. Her abnormally long arm stretched out in front, indicates a line that continues to infinity. This characteristically romantic pose expresses the final moment of hesitation before taking flight in the empyrean.

But this is mere technique. My intention was to bring about a " clearer understanding " of the " structural defects " of the Sylphide—defects which prove to be essential to the beauty of dancing.

This inquiry reminds me of a witticism attributed to M. Max Liebermann, the great impressionist painter of

Berlin. When an official drew his attention to Cezanne's *Garconnet au Gilet Rouge*, declaring that the arm was far too long, he retorted : " When an arm is painted in that manner it cannot be long enough." This reply bears on Taglioni's arm. The shortened trunk and the abnormal development of the legs predestined this dancer for travelling movements and *pas d'élévation*. Her covering power is enormous, the length of the spring enables her to leap into the air in a tremendous parabola. This is the way the grass-hopper is made and, if you will, the kangaroo. Nature, who thus equipped the insect and the ruminant, also made Taglioni, the dancer.

As soon as she touches the ground, she is vulnerable. In Nourrit's little plot, the Sylphide dies as her wings fall off. There is a lithograph of Chalon's that has caught, with an effect of foreshortening that anticipates Degas, a choregraphic curtsy of Taglioni. In this, where she bends her knees in the fourth position, the peculiarities of her physical structure are emphasised to the point of unintentional caricature.

Was this chosen of the gods, then, really a freak of nature ? Yes—just as all pure spirit changes when it becomes incarnate, like the four-handed Siva of the Hindus, the Ariel of Shakespeare, or the winged Eros of the ancients.

* * *

To write a poem, words are necessary. Whence did Taglioni derive her vocabulary? She adapted to her use the traditional language of the classic school. If she enriched it with a new play of fancy, she restricted or forbade the use of certain other choregraphic terms. Hence, if we may credit Charles Maurice, she created " not a manner, but a style."

Our authorities enable us to define this style. It favoured *form denuded of ornament*, big simple lines, sweeping trajectories. This saltatory plain-song renounced such grace notes as *batterie*, the swift impact of double *cabrioles*, the zigzag of the *entrechat* making a fantastic broken line while the dancer rises. Gyration is limited to some rare

MARIE TAGLIONI IN HER LAST YEARS

*From a photograph by Albert, London,
in the collection of Mlle. Derra de Moroda*

enveloping movement; never would the Sylphide be engulfed in the dionysiac fury of a series of *pirouettes*. The low and barbed *pointe* seems to perfect the vertical line of equilibrium, not to support the body in bold and varied *équilibres*. Moving with great bounds, she appeared to be suspended in the air, then sank to earth, hovering, when, like a spring-board, the resilient spring of her muscles impelled her into the air once more. This elasticity of knee and, above all, of instep, overcame weight, lessened the effect of gravitation, and enabled her to alight without the slightest noise. There is a story about her father's threatening to curse his daughter if he ever *heard* her dance.

These sustained and soaring flights corresponded to the slow progress of *développés* on the ground. The cautious raising of the *pointe* in a line with the shin, the *dégagé* of the leg, its passing to *grande seconde*, the twisting of the torso, gave birth to an *arabesque*, the supreme formula of a spiritualistic choregraphy which conveys the soul of dancing. A print, a miniature by the Russian artist Timm, shows us one of Taglioni's *arabesques penchées*, or rather an *attitude allongée*, to make use of the language of pedantry, because the dancer's hands are joined in an attitude of supplication.

However it may be, it was not what she did in conformance with tradition that impressed her contemporaries, but that in which she diverged from or surpassed them. "This manner of execution, at once brilliant and continuous, which had nothing in common with the *tours de force* of the classic school (so says Alphonse Royer, the historian and director of the Opéra), produced by its novelty a profound surprise." "The old school of *entrechats* and *ronds de jambe*," declares for its part the *Nouvelle Biographie Didot* (1865), which goes back to the seventeenth century, "was stricken to death by the novelty of her dancing." Nothing could be more erroneous than this judgment, but nothing is more indicative of the general blindness. If the "purist" happens to introduce some superfluity, some brilliant flourish into her dancing, astonishment is unanimous.

" I tell you, gentlemen, she did an *entrechat !* "
" Impossible ! Are you sure ? "
" Two *entrechats*, three *entrechats*."
This dialogue, recorded by Jules Janin in his account
of September 30th, 1833, proves the disconcern caused by
Taglioni's beating a *pas*. " She dances like all dancers
before her, and as others no longer dance after her ! "
The " lions " were moved by such a heresy as the heads
of the romantic school would have been at listening to
Théramène's recital. " Mlle. Taglioni is the George Monk
of the Opéra," concludes the journalist, " the classic dance
is indebted to her for its restoration."

In Taglioni's customary simplicity, in her renunciation
of the pomps and vanities of an elaborate and sophisticated
method of execution, eyes blinded by hate discovered many
weaknesses.

Charles Maurice, that traitorous panegyrist, went so far
as to refuse her all originality : " Mlle. Taglioni's success,"
insinuates the viperish critic, " originally founded on
incontestable merit and methods of execution which were
novel to those who did not know where this dancer had
slavishly copied them. . . . The continual recurrence of
five *temps*, of which the whole of this dance is composed,
soon exhausts attention." And resuming the supposed
statements of an important paper, he reproaches his victim
for her " academic poses, soft and languorous gestures,
affected balance, fanciful *entrechats* and *pirouettes*." Lastly,
on the very eve of her inexpressible triumph in *La Sylphide*,
the *Courrier des Théâtres* delivers a funeral oration over
this reign that has ended : " No balance, toes in the
air, beats of the knees, plenty of grimaces, *ungainliness*
and a great deal of charlatanism, that is what she shows
us."

Thus is presented, translated into the slang of the
" wings " and the language of envy, the inventory of the
Taglionesque style. But, truth to tell, the analysis of this
style can only be falsified by a purely technical and professional examination. That the existence of such astonishing harmony between the amplitude of movement

and the dancer's height had modified the aspect of certain conventional poses and *pas* is no more than an exterior sign of that *novelty* whose spirit we seek. Because it is not only a question of *craft*, but a manifestation of *style*. In the course of this study we have, on more than one occasion, attempted to define this style by setting the testimonies of eye-witnesses side by side. Let the "bourgeois of Paris," His Majesty Véron I (if it be not the "ghost" who wrote his *Memoirs*), recapitulate Taglioni's assets and her father's teaching :

"Like the artists of great periods of painting, Taglioni *père* founded a new school of dancing, very different from the style and philosophy governing that of Gardel and Vestris. Vestris taught grace and seduction ; he was a sensualist. . . . [Taglioni] demanded a graceful facility of movement, lightness, elevation above all, and *ballon* ; but he would not allow his daughter to make a single gesture or attitude lacking in decorum or modesty. He told her : 'Mothers and daughters should be able to see you dance without blushing.' . . . Vestris required pupils to dance as they did at Athens, like bacchantes and courtesans. Taglioni required of the dance an almost mystic and religious artlessness, while the other preferred a more catholic conception. But these transcendental *pas* and esoteric *cabrioles* had to be wrested from unwilling nature. Some idea of the daily labour imposed on the Sylphide by the well-meaning and implacable paternal tyranny may be gleaned from another passage in the same *Memoirs* : 'Abundant sweats, overwhelming hardships, tears— nothing softened the heart of that father, dreaming of glory for the talent that bore his name.' And Albéric Second, in his amusing *Petits Mystères de l'Opéra* says : 'I have seen Mlle. Taglioni, after her father had given her a two hours' lesson, almost drop dead on the carpet of her room, where she let herself be undressed, sponged and re-dressed, without seeming to know what was taking place."

When one is thus made aware of the price paid for that unfettered and ethereal mastery, one can no longer be astonished at the penury of the sentimental life of such a dancer, a willing martyr to her profession.

* * *

Did Taglioni's influence give an impetus to theatrical dancing ? It is a difficult question to answer. The Sylphide had enlarged the sphere of ballet by her conquest of the land of dreams. But genius not being transmissible, the whole burden of this spiritual royalty devolved on her frail shoulders. The spectacle as a whole was sacrificed to her creative personality ; the *corps de ballet* being reduced to a discreet accompaniment, the *ensemble* withered away. Taglioni was an *artist*, but she inevitably inaugurated the age of *virtuosi*.

A graver thing still, in causing the *eternal feminine* to triumph she evicted male dancing. The eclipse was complete. Not a single great male dancer arose between Perrot the Aerial and Nijinsky. "The male dancer has fallen into decline," says Saint-Léon. And he had been pre-eminent in the days of the Vestris ! "It may be said that to-day the male dancer exists no longer," observes Charles de Boigne in 1856. "A few years have sufficed to turn them into fossils . . . male dancers fill the posts of teachers, mimes or *maîtres de ballet*." Henceforth, what was expected of a Lucien Petipa, or a Mérante ? To serve as a living pivot for the *tours* of a *danseuse* and to "juggle not too clumsily with a hundred-pound weight." "We have suppressed male dancers," confirms Jules Janin.[1] When Guerra, a native of Milan and the best of the pupils of the great Carlo Blasis, who codified the classical ballet, took it into his head to come and dance at the Opéra, he was received with a storm of hisses, so unusual a spectacle had the male dancer become. In the Spanish ballet, *Paquita*, arranged by Mazilier, women dressed as men took part in the *Grand Pas des Gitanes*. This happened in 1846.

---

[1] The season of 1832, the year in which *La Sylphide* was produced, was fatal to male dancers, the disfavour in which they were held was such that their number was reduced, while that of the *danseuses* was increased, a measure which perpetuated the decline of the male dancer.

We find it curious that female characters should have been taken by men in the theatre of Shakespeare's day, or in the Nōh plays of Japan. But, even in our time, male characters in *Coppélia* or the *Deux Pigeons* continue, at the Opéra, to be taken by women, so that fantastic customs in matters of dancing die hard.

Thus did feminine romanticism lay waste the domain of ballet. The Taglionesque exaltation, hypertrophy of the soul, paved the way for a period of sterile virtuosity. A whole century had to pass ere another dancer of her rare quality came to add to the elegy of the *Sylphide* the nocturne of the *Mort du Cygne*.

CPSIA information can be obtained at www.ICGtesting.com
Printed in the USA
LVOW11s1332180216

475690LV00001B/38/P